THE WOMEN OF INDIA AND CHRISTIAN WORK IN THE ZENANA

THE WOMEN OF INDIA AND CHRISTIAN WORK IN THE ZENANA

MARY WEITBRECHT

GYAN

Published by

GYAN

Gyan Publishing House
5, Ansari Road
Daryaganj, New Delhi-110002
Phone: 011-47034999, 9811692060
E-mail: books@gyanbooks.com

Distribution Network
gyanbooks.com
India, USA, Canada, UK, Australia

ISBN: 978-93-7133-237-8 (HB)

First Published, 1875

2nd Impression 2025

Printed at: Gyan Press, Delhi.

THE WOMEN OF INDIA AND CHRISTIAN WORK IN THE ZENANA

Author: MARY WEITBRECHT

THE

WOMEN OF INDIA

AND

CHRISTIAN WORK IN THE ZENANA.

BY

MRS WEITBRECHT.

LONDON:
JAMES NISBET & CO., 21 BERNERS STREET.
MDCCCLXXV.

PREFACE.

The papers which compose this little book were prepared some time ago at the special request of the Rev. Dr Warneck of Barmen, and the Rev. Professor Christlieb of Bonn, Prussia, the editors of a monthly scientific review of missions throughout the world,*—and have been translated and published in German.

It was not intended to make further use of them, but one friend deeply interested in the subject wished the information contained in these papers to be given to the English public. Feeling that every effort we can make to impress our country-people with the importance of helping to raise the women of our Indian Empire to their right position is worth making, this request has been complied with. We might have added to the romance of the book by many more affecting details of conversions and personal incidents; but the subject of zenana visitation is still one that requires to be touched cautiously. The aim has been rather to embody as much

* A valuable magazine, to be obtained of Trübner & Co., Ludgate Hill, E.C. Subscription, 7s. per annum.

practical and historical information within a short compass as might tend to excite an increased and healthy interest in the minds of the readers. The book contains nothing which has not already appeared in print in some form or other. It is simply a compilation, consecutively arranged, of what is known to those who have looked into the subject, yet which should be known far more extensively.

The title of the German work is—

FRAUEN MISSION IN INDIEN.*

It forms one of a series entitled—

LEBENSBILDER AUS DER HEIDEN-MISSION.†

Intended by Dr Warneck to comprehend a complete history in brief of Foreign Missions.

M. WEITBRECHT.

LONDON, *April* 1875.

P.S.—Those who desire continuous information on the subject of this book, will find it in

THE FEMALE MISSIONARY INTELLIGENCER

(Suter & Co., 32 Cheapside); in

THE INDIAN FEMALE EVANGELIST

(Nisbet & Co., 21 Berners Street); and in the organs of the various societies alluded to in its pages. Subscriptions to those named 1s. per annum.

---

* Women's Mission in India.

† Life-Pictures from Missions to the Heathen.

CONTENTS.

BIOGRAPHIES.

THE WOMEN OF INDIA

AND

CHRISTIAN WORK IN THE ZENANA.

INTRODUCTION.

WE read, in the works of travellers and in the reports of missionaries, that the hundred millions of women of India have been kept for centuries, and are still kept, in a state of degradation resembling slavery, and that by consent of her priests and sages. The fact is startling to us, yet it is a fact based on evidence not to be gainsayed.

It was, however, not always so, though, apart from the influence of Christianity, Western usages ever allowed greater liberty to women than was accorded to them in the East. It will be interesting, as an introduction to the subject which follows, to trace some of the religious and political changes which have combined to produce this effect on the social condition of Hindu women.

We cannot fix the exact time when the Indian branch of the great Aryan family separated from its Iranian brother,—left their common home in the highlands of central Asia,—crossed the Hindu Kush, and began the conquest of Hindusthan. It seems unlikely to have been earlier than 2000 or later than 1500 B.C. Their first settlement was between the Sutlej and Jumna, in a district now known as Sersooty and Caggar, insignificant in point of size, but honoured as the classical land of the Aryan settlers. From this point they gradually advanced over the peninsula, and with their physical and mental superiority subdued the weaker aborigines, driving the more sturdy of them into the mountain regions, where they still remain.

The religion of these Aryans was a pure worship of nature: the shining heavens, fire, light, the storm wind, darkness, &c. These they personified and endowed with consciousness, power, and moral qualities. It was a most simple worship, performed not in temples, or at shrines, but on a rude altar in the open air, on which was placed their offerings of rice, butter, milk, &c., with the fermented juice of the acid asclepias to strengthen their good deities for battle against the evil demons. On special occasions animals were offered, sometimes even a horse. Hymns composed by seers (containing prayers and praises for temporal, moral, and religious blessings) were recited, and certain sacrificial sentences, but the whole might be performed by any father of a family. Literary monuments of these ancient times are preserved in the Vedas, the most ancient of which is the Rig Veda, compiled (we suppose) about 1100 B.C.

CHAPTER I.

THE SOCIAL CONDITION OF THE WOMEN OF INDIA IN THE EARLIEST AGES.

We will now consider the social condition of the women of India—

I. In the more settled *Vedic Age.*

II. In the *Heroic Age,* during which the wars of extermination were carried on against the aborigines; and

III. In the ascendant *Brahminic Age,* with which our time is connected.

I. *The Vedic Age.*—The Aryans were still during this age fresh from their ancestral home, and satisfied with their simple traditions brought thence with them to the regions along the Indus. While dwelling there they continued their pastoral life and patriarchal customs; the father was both parent and priest over his own household. Marriage was the union of one man to one woman for life. The mother was an important and influential person not only in the domestic, but in the religious life of the family. Hymns found in the Rig Veda show us that the normal idea of worship was, that it should proceed from a married couple, and the duality of the deities is applied as if corresponding with the marriage relation. Yet even here we find traces of polygamy among the higher classes, for one of the Vedic hymns alludes to "the husband of many maidens," and in another a young seer celebrates in rapturous strains the generosity of a Rajah, who has given him ten daughters in marriage.

These same hymns also contain traces of the more unnatural system of *polyandry*.* The twin brothers Aswin, probably the morning and evening stars, who usher in dawn and twilight, win a fair damsel, the prize in a chariot race, and are thus addressed:—"Aswins . . . . . The damsel who was the prize, acknowledges your husbandship, saying, 'You are my lords, &c.'" We cannot decide the length of the *Vedic Age*, but after generations these Aryans were pressed from behind, and moved southward on a career of conquest which ushers in—

II. *The Heroic Age.*—This gives us exaggerated stories in their epics of the wars of extermination; of might overcoming right, of the valour and heroic deeds of the subjugators, which are painted in glowing colours, while the poor aborigines are described as demons of darkness and cowardice. These poems open to us a vivid picture of the age they represent, and enable us to trace the origin of the hill tribes, such as the Kohls and Santhals, and in a more mixed condition the natives of the Dekhan; Telegus, Cana-

* This system is still prevalent in Upper Kanawar beyond the British territory. It has died out during the last fifty years within the boundary, through the influence of the British Government.

rese, Tamuls, &c. The chief of these poems are the "Mahabarat," or "Great War," and the "Ramayana," or "Adventures of Rama."

The *Heroic Age* reminds us in many respects of the age of Chivalry in Europe. In both the warrior class was dominant, and their energies chiefly directed to the spread of their religion and their national power, and in both *woman* exercised an immense influence and enjoyed much freedom.

As in Europe the knights contended for the favour of their ladies in tilts and tournaments, so in India there were public exhibitions in which the warriors displayed their prowess, and the seats around were occupied not only by Rajahs and other nobles, but by Ranis, Princesses, and ladies, splendidly dressed, who inspired the warriors with ardour.

The "Swayamvara," or "self-choice," alluded to in the Rig Veda, was in this age fully developed. When a father wished to give his daughter the choice of a husband, he invited a number of young men of rank and position to a festival, and she selected for herself the one she preferred, who, in return for the favour she conferred, made her the object of his true love. The story of "Nala and Damayanti" is a fine instance of this choice in its pure and primitive form. It is an exquisitely beautiful picture of womanly tenderness and devotion, of loving self-sacrifice and life-long fidelity, alike in prosperity and adversity. We give the story in brief:—

"When Bhima, the Rajah of Vidarbha, in Berar, sent Brahmans round the land to proclaim a Swayamvara, all the Rajahs, who had heard of the 'radiant charms and exceeding grace and loveliness' of his daughter, eagerly flocked to his court with all the pomp of chariots and horses, elephants and armies. Bhima welcomed them with royal courtesy, and entertained them with princely hospitality. Amongst them was Nala, King of Nashadha, in the Bhil country, a singularly 'handsome, brave, majestic, and splendid man, gifted with the choicest virtues, renowned for his skill in archery, and all other noble qualities and princely attainments.'

"Between him and the 'pearl of maidens,' from what they had heard, and, perhaps, in these days of greater freedom from what they had previously seen of each other, a mutual affection, deep and intense, had already sprung up. In some way which would shock the advocates of the rigorous seclusion of later times, when the bride is not allowed to see the husband who has been chosen for her, till the day of actual betrothal, Nala, without fear, or risk of challenge, entered the palace of Bhima, and finding ready access to the inner apartments, beheld the beautiful damsel seated among her maidens. Nala, 'radiant as the sun, and comely as the God of Love, smiled sweetly on Damayanti, and she, with lovely eyes, smiled sweetly in return.'

"A long and impassioned colloquy ensued, and then the royal maiden, with tearful eyes, fervently plighted her troth to Nala, protesting that she would choose no other lord than the hero who then stood before her, clenching her protest with these burning words :—'And if you spurn my love, I will take poison, or plunge into the water or the fire.'' At length the great day of the Swayamvara dawned upon the city of Vidarbha.

"And," as the old story runs, "all the Rajahs, sick with love, passed through the glittering portals and the court of golden columns, and entered the hall of state, like lions entering their mountain lairs. They were adorned with fragrant garlands, and rich ear-rings of costly gems were hanging in their ears. Some had long arms, robust and vigorous as the ponderous battle-mace, whilst others were as soft and delicately rounded as a smooth serpent, with bright, flowing hair, and arched eyebrows, their faces were as radiant as the stars; and they filled the hall of state as the serpents fill the under-world, or as tigers fill the caves in the mountains.

"But when Damayanti entered the hall, every eye was fixed, and every soul entranced at her dazzling loveliness; and all the Rajahs gazed with deep and passionate emotion on her surpassing beauty. Soon the name of every Rajah was proclaimed aloud, and Damayanti gazed around her at the glittering throng of suitors.

"At length, spying the object of her affection in the crowd, she, in all maidenly modesty, went up to him, took hold of the hem of his garment, threw round his neck a wreath of radiant flowers, and chose him for her lord. A sound of wild sorrow burst from all the Rajahs; but the gods and sages cried aloud, Well done! Then Nala, turning to the slender-waisted damsel, said:—'Since, O maiden with the eye serene, you have chosen me for your husband in the presence of the gods, know that I will be your faithful consort, ever delighting in your words, and as long as my soul shall inhabit this body I solemnly vow to be thine and thine alone!'

"Then, according to the usage of these primitive times, Rajah Bhima, acting not only as the head, but as the Priest of his own family, in his fatherly joy and pride, performed the marriage rites of his loving daughter and her chosen lord, and in due time Rajah Nala carried away his bride to his own city."

ANOTHER FORM OF THE SWAYAMVARA.

But there was another form of the Swayamvara, in which a damsel was bestowed as a prize on the warrior chief, who outdid all his rivals in feats of valour and skill, and thus bore more striking resemblance to the tournaments of the Middle Ages. The most notable instance of this is the story of Draupadi, the Rajah of Panehala.

"All the people," as the old story runs, "said that this damsel was the loveliest in all the world, and as radiant and graceful as if she had but just descended from the city of the gods, and that all the Rajahs from the four quarters of the earth would be present at the Swayamvara, and would seek to win her as a wife. Soon, around the city a vast number of Rajahs encamped, with a great host of troops and elephants, and multitudes of Brahmans, Khetriyas, travelling merchants, dancers and showmen, jugglers and musicians, actors and athletes, wrestlers and swordsmen; and a countless miscellaneous throng of spectators.

"And there was set apart, without the city, a large plain enclosed by barriers, in which the Rajahs were to exhibit their skill in archery, and around the plain were many glittering pavilions for the more distinguished guests, and also raised galleries from whence to behold the performances. At one end of the plain was a tall pole, on the top of which was a golden fish, and below the golden fish was a chakra (or large quoit) ever whirling round; the rule of the Swayamvara was, that whoever discharged an arrow through the chakra at the first shot, and struck the eye of the golden fish, that man should be the husband of the daughter of Rajah Draupadi.

"After sixteen days of sports and feasting, the morning of the Swayamvara dawned upon the city, and at the rising of the sun, gorgeous flags were waving in every quarter, and the city was awakened by the sounding of trumpets and beating of drums. Presently the Rajahs, too numerous to mention, took their appointed seats in the galleries; and there provisions of every sort were served to the guests; whilst cupbearers went round, distributing and sprinkling rosewater sandal and other odoriferous woods and sweet perfumes.

"After a while," as the narrative proceeds, "the moment arrived when the young princess was to exhibit herself in all her loveliness to those who hoped to gain her as a bride, dressed in elegant array, and adorned with radiant gems. She was led into the arena, carrying in her hand the garland she was to throw over the neck of the hero who might have the fortune to win her for his wife.

"Then the different choirs of Brahmans chanted Vedic hymns to the glory and praise of the gods; and filled the heavens and the earth with the music of their prayers. After this, and amidst the universal silence, the Prince Dhrishta-dyumna, who was the brother of Draupadi, stood by the side of his resplendent sister, and proclaimed that whoever shot the arrow through the chakra in the first attempt, and struck the eye of the golden fish, should have the princess for his wife.

"He then told into the ears of Draupadi the name and lineage of every one of her suitors; and he also told her, in the hearing of all, that she must place the garland round the neck of that man who struck the fish, and accept him for her husband on that day. Dhrishta-dyumna then turned to the Rajahs and chieftains, and said:—'Here stands this lady, my sister; whoever feels confident in his skill and strength to hit the mark in a single trial, let him arise and fulfil the conditions of the Swayamvara.'

"On the challenge being thus given, the Rajahs arose from their seats and approached the pole on which the golden fish was fixed; the chakra below was ever turning round; and they viewed the strong heavy bow from which the arrow was to be discharged.

"Now every man was jealous of the other; and yet,

for a long while, no chieftain would take up the bow, lest he should fail to bend it, and losing all chance of the coveted prize, excite the laughter and derision of the multitudinous host of spectators. Presently a Rajah ventured to step before his fellows, and tried to bend the bow, but could not, and another, and another, casting aside their robes and collars, and straining themselves to the uttermost, essayed in like manner to string the bow, but all were alike unable so to do because of its great size and strength.

"Then it was that Karna, an ambitious upstart of humble origin, but of great physical power, entered the arena, and to the surprise and dismay of all present, bent the bow and fitted the shaft to the string. It looked, therefore, as if he might successfully perform the crucial feat, which would proclaim him victor and winner of the incomparable prize.

"And here it is noteworthy that not the father of the maiden, not the brother, nor any other relative, or friend attempted to interpose. No; it was Draupadi herself, who, in her womanly pride and spirit of free and independent action, modestly but fearlessly stepped forward, and cried out with a loud voice, 'I wed not with the base born.' On which Karna, bursting with rage and bitterness, retired abashed.

"At last, after a considerable pause, Arjuna, one of the great Pandava chiefs, suddenly advanced from the crowd, and lifting the bow, bent it, drew the cord, and fitting the arrow to the string, he discharged it through the centre of the chakra and struck the eye of the golden fish. Then a roar of acclamations arose from that vast assembly, like the crash and roll of distant thunder, and the drums and trumpets filled the air with joyous music. Draupadi, filled with joy and wonder at the youth and grace of the hero who had struck the golden fish, came forward as she had been commanded by her brother, and threw the garland round the neck of Arjuna, and permitted him to lead her away, according to the rule of the Swayamvara."

Having thus illustrated this feature of the Heroic Age, we proceed to give an abstract of another legend; that of Sita, the ideal of Indian womanhood, and exercising an immense influence over the female mind of India, which has for its sole food the legends of Hindu mythology and history.

THE STORY OF SITA.

The story of Sita is contained in the Ramayana. In this and the Mahabharat we may study the Hindu character, just as we may that of the Greeks in their Iliad and Odyssey :—

Ianak, King of Mithila, being without family, sought by sacrifice to procure the gift of a son from the gods. As he was marking out a sacred spot for his altar with a plough, he found in the furrow an egg, whence sprung a female infant. The king adopted the child as his daughter, and gave her the name of Sita, "a furrow." She grew up the fairest of the fair, her goodness was equal to her beauty, and her mind equal to her goodness.

The time came when the King must find her a

husband, worthy of so much excellence and grace. But how shall he choose among rival claimants for her hand. The huge iron bow of the god Siva will supply a suitable means of testing the virtues of the Princes. The King makes proclamation that he only will be accepted, who can bend the bow of the dreadful Siva. The fame of Sita draws many a high-born youth, to come with pomp and display and to return ashamed. At length Rama, son of Dasaratha, King of Ayodhya, visited Mithila. He speedily bent and broke the iron bow, and was forthwith welcomed as the bridegroom worthy of Sita.

Happiness seemed now to be the lot of the Princess. Dasaratha, wearied with age and care, determined to resign his crown to Rama; and all Ayodhya was rejoicing in the prospect of the new reign, when an incident happened which menaced the whole scheme, and threw before Rama the opportunity of noble but painful virtue, instead of the glory of the promised crown.

One of the king's wives, in return for faithful and affectionate service, had received promise of such a gift as she should choose to demand; waiting with the patience of a Hindu the long-deferred moment of advantage, she found at last this happy crisis, and claiming from the king the boon he had freely offered, demanded that Rama should be banished to the forest of Dandaka for fourteen years, and the crown given to her son Bharat. In vain the aged monarch sought to turn her from her purpose; no threat, no entreaty availed.

The King was compelled to appeal to Rama, who instantly recognised his duty. Dearer to his pure soul was his father's honour than all his father's kingdom. He cheerfully resigned the crown, and bent his every effort to the complete fulfilment of the King's promise. This is the first great moment of the story. The interest of it is centred upon Rama, whose character comes out nobly under the trial; the one great principle of filial obedience enabling him to resist the fond sophistry of his own mother, and all the other influences which could assail a generous soul at such a time.

Presently Sita appears, and the interest of the story fastens upon her. Rama, either to try her affection or sincerity, proposes that she should remain in the capital while he wanders in the far-off forest, and he sets forth the manner of the conduct he would have her pursue in his absence. She, however, rejects with scorn his proposal, and determines to share his exile. He seeks to dissuade her by picturing the hardships she must meet, but to no purpose; she entreats:—

> "Oh let me go; whate'er I may endure,
> Following thee will make my soul more pure;
> So joy shall crown me in the after life,
> For thou art God unto thy loving wife."

And again—

> "With thee is heaven, where'er thou art not—hell;
> Oh lead me hence, that I in heaven may dwell;"

though heathen-like she adds—

> "But if thou wilt to no entreaties bend,
> Poison, or flood, or flame my life shall end."

He yields at last :—

> "He gently held her, raised her drooping head,
> And stayed the sweet soul that had well-nigh fled:
> 'Not heaven shall bribe me from my wife to part.'"

We must not stay to describe the various scenes in which the farewell and the departure from the royal city are described, nor yet the events of their journey into exile, accompanied by Rama's brother Lakshman.

At times the exiles enjoy the beauty of the woods, and Rama delights to point out the charms of the landscape, exclaiming at last,—

> "O Sita, I am wild with joy,
> So rare a lot is mine,
> Cheered by a duteous brother's care,
> And loved with love like thine."

But such simple joys cannot last; not for such happiness has Rama been born.

The great purpose of his life is now to be accomplished, and to this end he must lose Sita. Ravan, the mighty and monstrous King of Ceylon, determines to possess himself of her. A deer of marvellous beauty draws Rama away into the depths of the forest. Lakshman keeps watch at home, till presently he hears his brother's voice: "O Lakshman, save me!" He doubts for a moment whether to obey the call, or maintain his watch; but Sita urges him to hasten to her husband's assistance; at length he leaves her.

The plots of Ravan have prevailed; the deer and the voice are a delusion for which she has been fatally forsaken. Ravan appears and carries her off to Ceylon.

The poem now describes, on the one side, the faithfulness of Sita in her terrible imprisonment, and on the other, the resolute persistence of Rama in waging a fearful war with Ravan for her deliverance. The monkey gods assisting him, he builds the causeway across the Straits of Manaar, the remains of which we call Adam's Bridge. And after a series of appalling conflicts, full of adventure and strange incident, in which the presence of the monkeys provides a monstrous mirth, Ravan is slain and Sita rescued. This might seem a fit end for the story of their love; but the terrible Ramayan has new sorrows for them.

The question now arises whether Rama may take back the Sita he had so long lost, and for answer she accepts a fiery ordeal. She enters a fierce furnace, which has no power upon her; and she is received with acclamations as the faithful and altogether worthy wife of Rama, who had demanded this ordeal with the same unrelenting conscience which had accepted exile for himself at his father's bidding.

Again the sunshine of prosperity shines upon the pair. The fourteen years of exile are past, and they return with great triumph to Ayodhya. The whole kingdom rejoices. Bharat, who had placed Rama's shoe upon the throne beneath the royal umbrella, and contented himself with reigning in its behalf, welcomes back his loved brother, and the golden happiness in which stories ought to end seems secure; but no, it may not be, the stern Ramayan is not yet satisfied.

One day Rama discovered that his kingdom was not as prosperous as he could wish. Pressing his ministers to explain the cause, one of them at length had the courage to tell him that the fault lay with himself, that it was not sound morality to take back, solicited by his own private affection, the Queen who had been so many months in the dungeons of his enemy. This startled the King, and an incident which presently followed, deepened the impression it produced.

As he passed to his bath in one of the royal ponds, he overheard two washermen quarrelling. "What," says one, "your father was such a respectable, well-behaved man, that I did not hesitate to give you my daughter, but you have beaten her so cruelly that she has run home to us. Now it is against all the Shastras that she should stay with us."

To this the other replied: "Your daughter does not want to live with her husband; she has run away from her husband's house. How can I take her back? Rama took back Sita after she had been in Ceylon, to be sure, but Rama is a King, and can do as he likes; but if we poor folk were to do the same we should be disgraced in the eyes of our neighbours."

Other circumstances lent weight to these indications of popular feeling, and Rama, esteeming kingly duty his highest responsibility, took advantage of a desire Sita expressed to visit the forest of her exile, and sent her thither under the escort of one of his brothers, who on her arrival announced the King's command that she should never return to court. Her grief at this terrible news was almost equalled by Rama's, as he meditated on the woful sacrifice public duty had demanded of him. He caused a golden image of his wife to be made, by which he at once solaced and tortured his affections.

Not yet, however, has the story ended. In her exile Sita gave birth to twin sons, and found in them some consolation under her banishment.

With the aid of the hermits in the wilderness, she trained them up in all excellent knowledge and in all skill of arms. By their means, at last, she was again remembered at the court, and Rama eagerly sent for her; but once more, on her arrival, he preferred public duty to private affection, and again sternly demanded the ordeal of fire. Sita refuses this demand, with pathetic dignity, and then, bursting out in a passion of grief, she relates her wrongs, and finally, accusing herself of being the cause of sorrow and trouble to her husband instead of joy, she appeals to the earth from which she originally sprang to receive her again into its bosom, and to the horror and amazement of the assembly, falls upon the ground dead.

Such is the story of Sita, the faithful wife, virtuous rather than happy; whose goodness receives a woman's reward, triumphant vindication of character through much suffering, even to death. Rama did not long survive her, and though he left sons to inherit his fame and kingdom, they cannot console us for the loss of Sita.

This poem is a tragedy. The legend of Savitri, as contained in thc Mahabharat, has a more cheerful issue.

CHAPTER II.

THE STORY OF SAVITRI AND INSTITUTES OF MANU.

As Wapati was the King of Madra (the ancient name of Bhûtan), and had only one child, Savitri, a daughter of his old age. She grew up the light of his heart, and at last the period arrived of giving her in marriage; but no neighbouring prince wooed her—all were too dazzled by her beauty to come near.

So since, in point of fact, she had received no proposals for marriage, the father told her that she might choose a husband for herself. Accordingly the King sent her one day to pay a visit to the neighbouring hermitages. Near one of these she saw, in the act of playing with the sons of the Rishis, or holy sages, Satyavan, son of Dyumatsena, the old King of Avanti, who had become blind and lost his kingdom, and was now living with his family in retirement in the depths of the forest.

Savitri, having very closely noted his varied movements, and made searching inquiries concerning him, made up her mind that he should be her future husband. On her return she finds her father in deep conversation with a holy sage named Narada. As she enters the room the sage asks why she is still unmarried, and in the course of the conversation, Savitri discloses that her heart is given to Satyavan. Narada exclaims: "Alas! alas! Great is her error that she has chosen in her ignorance the virtuous Satyavan." The King anxiously asks the reason, but in answer to his inquiries Narada only repeats the Prince's good qualities, his beauty, modesty, gentleness, and learning—everything, in short, which could justify her choice. At length he adds:

> "Yet one cloud upon his virtues makes them profitless, O king,
> 'Tis a fault he ne'er can master by severe endeavouring—
> Subject to one shade, O monarch—only one, his virtues lie;
> In a year from this day counting, Satyavan shall surely die."

The King entreats his daughter to choose some other husband, but Savitri declares her heart is given irrevocably; and Narada, on hearing her resolve, advises her father to yield, as no other living man has Satyavan's virtues.

The marriage is soon arranged, and Savitri goes to live in the hermitage with her husband and his aged father and mother:

> "All the gems that decked her beauty she put off in lowliness,
> And her gentle limbs she covered with a hard, rough hermit dress;
> By her meekness and affection, by her ministering care,
> Did the sweet, contented lady win the heart of each one there."

Day by day, however, the time ran on in the quiet hermitage duties, until only three days remained of the fated period. Savitri, who had hid the dark secret close in her own bosom, now determined to spend those last days in a strict fast; and her father-in-law, who little guessed her real reason, in vain endeavoured to dissuade her.

The last morning at length dawned, and Satyavan took his axe on his shoulder and prepared to set out to the forest; but Savitri, for the first time since their marriage, begged him to allow her to accompany him. He at first objected, as her strength, weak with fasting, would be unable to endure the fatigues of the rough forest journey; but at length he yielded, and they set out together.

On every side, with wide-opened eyes, she beheld the various pleasant woods filled with flocks of peacocks, and the sacred flowing rivers, and the stately trees in full flower; and at every step Satyavan cried: "Look, look," in his pleasant voice. But ever as she looked at her husband she remembered the sage's words, and regarded him as already dead. With her gentle steps she went on following him, but her heart was cleft in twain as she thought of the time.

At length they reach the appointed spot, and Satyavan gathers a basket full of fruit and then begins to cut wood. As he is cutting, a violent pain suddenly arises in his head, and he comes back to Savitri, and wishes to sleep as he feels unable to stand. "She took his head on her lap and sat down on the ground, and, pondering the sage's words, she put together that minute, that hour, and that day."

At length she beholds an awful form standing beside her, clothed in red garments and with a noose in his hand, looking stedfastly on Satyavan, and feeling instinctively who it is, she lays her husband's head on the ground and rises, folding her hands in reverence. The stranger is Yama, the king of death, who proceeds to draw out the soul from the body, binding it in his noose. He then takes his way toward the south, and Savitri follows in silent sorrow. We extract in full the beautiful dialogue which takes place between them, when Yama at last bids her turn back :—

" Nay, but go thou back, Savitri, and his funeral rites prepare ;
Far as faithful wife should follow, thou hast followed, lady fair."

Savitri.

" Wheresoe'er my husband goeth, in the way where he is led,
There Savitri, faithful ever, still unfalteringly will tread ;
For my penance' sake and duty to my elders that I show,—
Wifely love and thine own favour, oh! forbid me not to go !
Him that goes seven paces with us truthful sages call a friend,
Thus I claim thy friendship, Yama ;—I will speak, do thou attend.
Led by love of truth and duty to the woods the wise repair,
And they speak because they know ; the fool—what business hath he there ?
Let but one man speak of duty, all true hearts his words obey,
And no second proof we need to make us follow in the way.
Duty swayeth the true-hearted, therefore, as the wise account,
Duty is the noblest motive, duty aye is paramount."

Yama.

" Thy sweet speech has charmed me, lady, and a boon to thee I give ;
I will grant whate'er thou askest, saving that thy lord may live."

Savitri.

" In the hermit grove, neglected, reft of kingdom, reft of sight,
Let my husband's sire recover vision and his royal right."

Yama.

" Yea, this boon I grant thee, lady, it shall be as thou dost pray,
But return thou home, Savitri, lest thou faint upon the way."

Savitri.

"Can I faint when near my husband? where he goes my path shall be;
I will follow where thou leadest,—listen once again to me.
He that to all living creatures nought but loving kindness shows,
Has the truest, best religion,—good men pity e'en their foes."

Yama.

"Sweet as water to the thirsty, lady! are thy words to me;
Ask again, his life excepted, gladly will I grant it thee."

Savitri.

"Heirless is the king my father, let a hundred sons of fame,
Duly born unto the monarch, spread the glories of his name."

Yama.

"Lady! it shall be unto him even as thy wishes are,
But return—thy prayer is granted; Princess, thou hast travelled far."

Savitri.

"'Tis not far, for *he* is near me—further, further speeds my mind;
Onwards! I will speak, O Yama! let my words a hearing find.
Resteth more upon the righteous than on self man's confidence,
Therefore seeketh each the worthy's friendship and benevolence;"
Gladly to the good and holy all their trusting love they give,
Boundless is the good man's kindness, for he loveth all that live.

Yama.

"Thou hast spoken well and wisely,—never yet spake woman so;
To my soul thy words are pleasant,—ask another boon and go!"

Savitri.

"Grant that many a prince, O Yama, I to my Satyavan may bear,
To uphold his house for ever, mighty, virtuous, and fair."

Yama.

"Many a son, fair, good, and mighty, lady! shall of thee be born;
But return, thy home is distant, faint art thou and travel-worn."

Savitri.

"Nay, the good ne'er cease well-doing, and they know not weariness.
Never is their meeting fearful, never is it profitless;
Great are they, the sun in heaven guide they by their truth and worth,
And bear up by their devotion this vast dwelling-place the earth;
Never when the good are near them do the good faint wearily,
For the good uphold for ever all that has been and shall be."

Yama.

"Just and sweet thy words are, true one,—ask, and I will not refuse
(So my soul is pleased with thee), any boon that thou shalt choose."

Savitri, at once, overjoyed, asked her husband's life; and on Yama's departure she hastened to the spot where the dead body lay, and sat down on the ground, taking the head in her lap. After a while Satyavan awakes as from a heavy sleep—"I have slept a long time, Savitri. Why didst thou not wake me? and who was that dark man who seemed to be dragging me away?" Savitri endeavours to conceal what has happened, and presses him to rise and go home.

"I will tell thee all to-morrow, rise now and hasten to thy parents. The night is deep round us, and the sun is gone, and the wild beasts of the forest are roaming abroad. I hear the rustle of the leaves, as the beasts wander among the trees, and yonder jackals howl, in the south-western quarter, shaking my inmost soul."

Satyavan doubts whether they shall be able to find their way through the forest in the darkness;

but Savitri remembers that she had seen, as they came in the morning, a dry tree, which was smouldering from some recent conflagration in the forest. From it she now procures a light, and they then proceed towards their home. The basket and wood they leave till to-morrow, but Savitri carries the axe in one hand, and supports her husband with the other.

In the meantime, great had been the consternation in the hermitage, as hour after hour passed and the pair had not returned. The old hermit-king had suddenly recovered his sight during the day, in consequence of Yama's boon, and he and his wife at last set out in search of them.

They went to the various hermitages and rivers, to the woods and lakes; they wandered by night seeking for their children. At every sound they heard they lifted up their heads, thinking that it was their son, and they said to each other, "Here comes Satyavan with Savitri." With their feet wounded by briars, and covered with blood, onward they rushed through the bushes, bewildered by terror.

The other hermits at last follow them, and persuade them to return to their cottage, assuring them that their children were really safe; and towards morning Savitri and her husband return. She then opens her full heart and tells them all her story.

The next day, messengers come from Dyumatsena's kingdom, to tell him that the usurper had been slain, and that his subjects were impatient for his return, even though he was blind. They find to their joy that the old King's sight is restored, and they all return at once in a triumphal procession to the capital. "Thus herself, her father, her mother, her father-in-law, her mother-in-law, and her husband's family, all these did Savitri by her virtue lift up from calamity."

On comparing both these legends with the great Homeric epic, we are struck by the fact that the leading personage is a *faithful* instead of a *faithless* WIFE.

In accordance with the more religious character of the former poem, we are told that Rama and his three brothers and wife are incarnations of the god Vishnu, born for the purpose of destroying the monster Ravan, who was to perish by human hands; reminding us of the "woman's seed," who was to bruise the serpent's head.

But this does not destroy the human interest of the story. Rama's high position and moral sensibility bring about a conflict of public and private duties; while Sita (and Savitri likewise) has but one life-principle for her guidance,—duty to her husband; and the conflict between this and injured affection brings about the catastrophe of the poem. Only at the last moment is there room for two opinions, and she chooses at any cost to herself the course which may best maintain her husband's dignity. "Thou art God unto thy loving wife," says Sita to Rama, and similar is the purport of Savitri's pleading with Yama for her husband's life

This is at once the strength and the weakness of

the ideal Hindu woman. We cannot but admire the beautifully unselfish devotion to the partner whom she has chosen; but untempered as it is by a reciprocal acknowledgment of her own claims on his part;—knowing no higher authority than his, she must put him in a false position, and sink with him when he falls from his unduly exalted pedestal.

The principle of unquestioning obedience, embodied in these poems, has continued most rigorously to be applied to the conjugal relation in India, and has brought about the enslavement of women which we shall soon come to consider.

We now turn from our delineation of the bright side of Indian womanhood during the Heroic Age, to speak of its darker aspect.

We meet (though this probably existed in the Vedic Age too) with instances of maidens being purchased with jewels or money, of marriages arranged by parents without regard to the feelings of bride or bridegroom,—of temporary alliances hallowed by no nuptial tie,—of damsels forcibly carried away in time of peace,—of a young and favourite wife consumed on the funeral pile of her husband,—and all this without particular censure, much as a matter of course.

To say nothing of other practices and forms of intercourse too gross to be enumerated, which are connived at, or even sanctioned, we note a progress in the demoralising institutions of *polygamy* and *polyandry*. The leading personages in the two mighty dramas already mentioned, are polygamists, amongst others Dasaratha, the Maharajah of Ayodhya, and father of Rama, is described as having three wives.

And as regards *polyandry*, we find that the eldest of a number of brothers was considered to be entitled to select and marry a damsel, who should be the joint wife of himself and his younger brethren; a right so indisputable that it might even override the prior claim of a victor at the Swayamvara. Thus Draupadi, whose choice has been related, was claimed by Yudhisthira, the eldest brother of Arjuna, and was married successively to the five Pandava brethren. Nor is this plural marriage an interpolation; on the contrary, it is one of the main incidents upon which the tragedy of the "great war" hinges; and ever and anon it again comes to the forefront.

During this period, of course, the Kshatrias, or military class, had been most prominent. Meanwhile, as new kingdoms were founded and great cities built, the simple religious institutions of the patriarchal age were supplanted by a regular priesthood. It was no longer possible for the head-man of the community to perform the increasingly complicated religious rites, and his place was taken by regular ministers of religion, who gradually consolidated into the Brahmana caste, so called because its members devoted themselves to Brahman, *i.e.*, sacred worship, or meditation (the name was not applied to the god till later).

This is the holiest of all the castes; next to it in point of distinction come the Kshatrias; then the Vaishyas, or agriculturists, and last the unclean

Shudras. Below the lowest come the outcast Pariahs (mountain dwellers). These castes have infinitely multiplied through subdivision: their complete development brings us down to—

THE AGE OF ASCENDANT BRAHMANISM.

Having become the depositaries of religious tradition, and the mediators between the people and their deities, their influence gradually increased, till at length they had enclosed the nation in a network of religious observances, extending to the inward impulses no less than to the outward movements. This they accomplished by a finely calculated adaptation and arrangement of the ancient religious records, to suit their own aims and purposes.

During this period it probably was that the laws of Manu (*i.e.*, the first man Adam) originated, though they were further Brahmanised and brought into their present form at a later period. In India, no one is ambitious of the honour of producing anything new, hence the title under which the compiler of this law code has concealed himself; meanwhile, it is not always easy to say what is original and what of later date. We may, however, suppose that the code of Manu represents the actual institutions of Indian life, as they had consolidated during this period, and were restored with increased strictness after the expulsion of Buddhism. The following points we may consider as characteristic of the condition of women during this age :—

The system of polyandry as a legitimate mode of marriage is not alluded to in this code; we therefore conclude that it gradually fell out of use, as the ascendancy of the Brahmans increased. The same may be said of the chivalrous institution of the Swayamvara. Its mention is studiously omitted in the institutes of Manu. It is the father who has to arrange a match for his daughter. The last remnant of independence in woman is taken away, and she is made utterly subordinate to the will of another. Instead of being a help-meet for man she is merely his slave.

"A girl," says Manu, "or young woman, must do nothing according to her own pleasure, even in her own dwelling-place. In childhood she is dependent on her father; in youth on her husband; in widowhood on her sons. If she has no sons, she must be dependent on the kinsmen of her deceased husband; if he left no kinsmen she must be dependent on the kinsmen of her father; if she have no such kinsmen she must be dependent on the Rajah. A woman must never seek to be independent. She must never wish to separate herself from her father, her husband, or her sons; for by such separation she exposes both her father's family and her husband's family to contempt."

What a striking commentary on the original sentence of condemnation pronounced at the Fall!

Not only is the first important step in life—that of marriage—entirely under the control of the father, but that bane of Hindu society, marriage in actual childhood, is enjoined. "Every man," says Manü, "should give his daughter in marriage to an excellent and handsome youth of the *same caste, even though she has not attained her age*, i.e., *eight years.* Once married, her sole duty is unquestioning obedience and fidelity; and this is held to be a full substitute for the dereliction of all other duties whatsoever.

"The husband," says Manu, "to whom her father has given her, or to whom her brother has given her with the consent of her father, she must obsequiously honour while he lives, and never neglect when he dies. The husband gives bliss continually to his wife here below, and he will give her happiness in the next world. He must be constantly revered as a god by a virtuous wife, even though he does not observe approved usages, or is enamoured of another woman, or is devoid of good qualities. No sacrifice is allowed to women apart from their husbands; no religious rite, no fasting,—so far only as a woman honours her lord, so far is she exalted in heaven."

What a singular paraphrase on the words of the original sentence, "Thy desire shall be unto thy husband, and he shall rule over thee!"

The germs of the zenana system, that is to say, the principle that it is needful to seclude woman by confinement from the outer world, are to be found in this code.

It speaks thus:—

"Husbands," says he, "should diligently keep their wives under lawful restrictions. No man, indeed, can restrain women by lawful measures; but a wife may be employed in purification and female duty, in the preparation of daily food and in the superintendence of household utensils. Women are not secure by confinement at home, even under affectionate and observant guardians. Through their evil passions, their mutable temper, their want of settled habits, they are always prone to go astray. Though monogamy is the rule, yet in frequent cases polygamy is sanctioned, and divorce is rendered easy for various reasons."

"A wife," says Manu, "who neglects her husband, though he be addicted to gaming, or fond of spirituous liquors, or diseased, must be deserted for three months, and deprived of her ornaments and household furniture. A wife may at all times be superseded by another wife, if she drinks spirituous liquors, or acts immorally, or shows hatred toward her husband, or is diseased, or mischievous, or wastes his property. A wife who is barren may be superseded in the tenth year; she who brings forth only daughters may be superseded in the eleventh year; but she who speaks unkindly may be superseded without delay."

In most cases the husband had the option of divorce, or of taking another wife, and thus practically setting the first one aside. But servility during life does not preclude a woman from obligation to her husband after death. Re-marriage is prohibited in the most solemn manner.

"When a husband," says Manu, "is dead, let his

widow emaciate her body by living voluntarily on pure flowers, roots, and fruit; but let her not even pronounce the name of another man. Let her continue until death, forgiving all injuries, performing harsh duties, avoiding every sensual pleasure, and cheerfully practising the incomparable rules of virtue, which have been followed by such women as were devoted to one husband alone. A virtuous wife ascends to heaven, though she have no child, if after the death of her husband she devotes herself to pious austerities. But a widow who, from a desire to bear children, slights her deceased husband by marrying again, brings disgrace upon herself below, and will be excluded hereafter from the seat of her lord."

And as if all this were not enough, the most deprecatory sentiments are throughout the code expressed relative to women, and the most contemptuous epithets applied to them. They are constantly ranked with the inferior castes. They are represented as incorrigibly fickle and frail, vicious and perverse, surcharged with all manner of hateful passions and impure desires. Of them it is positively affirmed that no confidence can ever be placed in them. We may trust deadly poison, a swollen river, a hurricane, the large fierce elephant, the tiger come from prey, the angels of death, a thief, a savage, a murderer, but a *woman never*. Consequently a creature so low, so degraded, so incurably depraved, can only be checked or restrained by correspondingly ignominious chastisement. "For *women*," says Manu, "children, persons of crazy intellect, the old, the poor, the infirm, the king shall order punishment with a small whip, a twig, or a rope." Again, "A wife, a son, a servant, a pupil, and a younger whole brother, may be corrected, when they commit faults, with a rope or a small shoot of a cane."

This position of woman in the social scale, as destined for nought else than to minister to the necessities of man in the household, precludes her from anything like mental cultivation, which would of necessity unfit her for mere drudgery such as this. Her essential inferiority is stamped with a perpetual brand by her exclusion from any occupation with the sacred books. "Women have no business with the text of the Vedas: this is the law fully settled; having therefore no evidence of law and no knowledge of expiatory texts, sinful women (*i.e.*, *all* women) must be foul as falsehood itself, and this is a fixed rule." For whereas the sciences in general, such as pronunciation, grammar, versification, arithmetic, &c., were all included amongst the sacred writings, women (and Shudras) being debarred from one, were likewise shut out from the other. Too true is the bitter saying of a Hindu lady, "Ignorance is the ornament of women in India."

Eventually, however, the oppressive tyranny exercised by the Brahmans over the religious and social life of the nation produced its reaction. In the sixth century before Christ there appeared a reformer, Cakya Muni, better known as Gouta Buddha, who, though a Prince by birth and education, renounced all worldly joys, and lived with his disciples an ascetic life, devoted himself to relieving the wants of the poor and needy outcasts, proclaiming the abolition of that barrier of caste which seemed to exclude them from the pale of humanity; a release from the intolerable round of outward observances and rites, and an era of religious liberty and equality.

This self-denying love to his fellow-creatures, and sympathy with the misery of life, drew to him thousands who understood nothing of his metaphysical theorems about unconscious absorption into the Niwana (=extinction or the transmigration of souls). The Brahmans began to notice and oppose him; but his doctrine spread like wildfire, eventually overrunning India and Ceylon, and extending far beyond their boundaries.

For the space of a thousand years Brahmanism lay in the dust, crushed, but not extinct, till at length in the sixth century of the present era it once more raised itself, and exterminated its adversary throughout the peninsula. Brahmanism was re-established; and now systematically organised, so as to place the nation more entirely than ever under the dominion of the priestly caste. This brings us down to the last period—

THE PURANIC AND PRESENT AGE.

This has its name from the Purannas, that enormously voluminous collection of writings in which is contained the remodelled mythology of India, as it has obtained during the last thousand years.

The Vedas, though adored, have become practically obsolete, since only the learned (and few enough of these) are at all thoroughly acquainted with their language. The Institutes of Manu and the whole religion have become intensely Brahmanised; though not without some traces of Buddhistic tenets. Foremost amongst these, and most important for our subject, is the transmigration of souls, inasmuch as it is now employed to account for the despite done to woman. Amongst those who are disgraced in this life, on account of sins committed in a former existence, are "the diseased, the maimed, *women* and infidels."

The form which the code of Manu took after the revival of Brahmanism, has effectually stereotyped the condition of woman in India down to the present day (with the exception, of course, of certain external ameliorations introduced by British rule); so that for all practical purposes the Purannic is equivalent to the present age.

Nor did the Mussulman rule in India apparently produce much alteration in this respect; for Halhed's code of Gentoo law, drawn up by a council of learned Brahmans at the request of Warren Hastings, and considered as a standard work in this branch, is for the most part either literally, or in substance, taken from the Institutes of Manu, with but few additions from other great legal authorities in accordance with its spirit. And what is especially to the purpose here, it deliberately reproduces the harsh sentiments and enactments of Manu with respect to womankind, as may be seen by the following specimen:—

"A man, both day and night, must keep his wife so much in subjection that she by no means be mistress of her own actions; if the wife have her own free will, notwithstanding she be sprung from a superior caste, she will yet behave amiss. A woman shall never go out of the house without the consent of her husband; and shall never hold converse with a strange man, and shall not stand at the door, and must never look out at the window; shall not eat till she has served her husband and his guests with victuals"—in a word, shall act in all things "according to the orders of her husband." *

We now proceed to describe the condition of women in India at the present day.

* Some valuable papers, contributed by Dr Duff and others to the early numbers of "The Indian Female Evangelist," have been very helpful in compiling these chapters.

CHAPTER III.

CONDITION OF WOMEN AS IT ACTUALLY EXISTS IN BENGAL AND NORTH-WEST INDIA.*

THE valley of the Ganges is the stronghold of Hinduism, and it is there that the seclusion of the higher born females is complete. The system obtains more or less all over India, but in a modified way in the southern and western provinces. It is to the presidency of Bengal our present description most exactly applies. The Hindu lady has often been spoken of as a prisoner, which in point of fact she has hitherto been. Happily we can now speak of her as a "*prisoner of hope*," for though our sketch of her position still applies to the majority of households, there are some where light and joy have entered through the zenana teacher.

There is a familiar saying, that when an infant, the Bengali woman should be under the guardianship of her parents; when young, under the control of her husband; and when old, under the care of her own offspring—at no period of her life is she mistress of herself.† Hers is, therefore, a threefold life: first,

* This chapter has appeared in "The Indian Female Evangelist."

† See page 31, second paragraph, for the origin of this saying.

as an infant; secondly, as a wife; and thirdly, as a mother.

Her early life is one, perhaps, of less trouble and anxiety than that of most girls. She is for the first eight or nine years of her existence a gay and thoughtless being; childish play is her delight. She dresses her dolls as it suits her fancy, after the fashion of either sex; she contracts mock relationships with her little earthen images, and may be seen fondling them as a young wife fondles the child in her arms; she marries her dolls, and her parents supply her with money to defray the expenses of the mock wedding. In a certain wealthy family in Calcutta, the expense of a single doll marriage amounted to some thousands of rupees. On the nature of the active sports of these little ones we will not enter here.

But at no stage of her life is the Bengali woman permitted to enjoy the inestimable benefits of education. Knowledge is as effectually closed upon her as the light of day is from the born blind. The education of female children does not come within the category of duties, as enumerated in the Shastras, which a father owes to his daughters; letters and knowledge are considered as incompatible with such a position as that of the woman in the social circle.

She does not, however, grow up without some sort of education, but it is simply that which has reference to domestic duties and religious observances, learning to perform the *brottos* or adorations, which belong to childhood. These brottos form no part of the Shastras, but are the inventions of the women themselves. They have peculiar names given them which convey no meaning, but a Bengali girl's hopes of earthly enjoyment and final beatitude are founded on them; she worships the god Shiva, that she may, through his favour, obtain a good husband, as good as Shiva himself was to his own beloved wife Parbutty.

Her accomplishments at this period consist in knowing how to twine strings of hair, which are made use of as a head-dress, and in painting with a white liquid, prepared of powdered rice, figures, on a wooden ground, or on the wall and floor of a room, that to a stranger will appear perfectly meaningless, but which to her are highly important signs and symbols.

As long as she is unmarried, no particular care is bestowed upon her by her parents as to her dress and personal embellishments, which become matters of importance to her when settled in life. This settlement is often sadly, even ridiculously premature, for, if circumstances occur to render it desirable, she is married at three or four years old, or even younger. There are instances of babes still in arms being married, and no sooner, however, does she attain the age of eight or nine, than the solicitude of her father increases as to how he shall dispose of her in marriage.

A daughter's marriage is not only a drain on the finances of a Bengali, but considerations of family honour are involved, and the choice of a worthy bridegroom is an object of extreme importance. He therefore sends for the Ghutakas, or persons employed to negotiate such affairs, and after the match is proposed by them, a day is fixed by the parent of the bridegroom, for the purpose of seeing the destined bride of his son. The parent himself, or some near relative on whose report he can place reliance, is accompanied by the Ghutaka on the appointed day to the house of the bride's father, by whom all necessary preparations are made for the reception of his guest. In a similar way the father of the bride returns the visit at the house of the bridegroom's father, where he examines the qualifications of his would-be son-in-law.

Thus the choice is made up on both sides, and after many preliminary engagements, which are done in writing, to make binding the match, a day which the Brahmans have appointed as auspicious is fixed for the celebration of the nuptial ceremony.

At length the moment of departure arrives, and the mother-in-law, for the only occasion that she is permitted by the custom of the nation to look her son-in-law in the face, takes him by one of his hands, and joining it with that of her daughter, pronounces a benediction on the young couple.* She gives her farewell to her child with tears in her eyes, and the rest of the family partake in the general sorrow. The scene is truly affecting and peculiarly Indian.

* This is the orthodox rule, but there are doubtless exceptional cases, and since so many houses have been opened by the zenana teachers, a relaxing influence has become apparent in some of the strict Hindoo observances.

The lament of parents at the departure of their daughters may not be to our taste, but it is perfectly natural in Hindu life.

Thus is this poor little girl torn away at a tender age from the home of her infancy to reside among strangers. She never saw before this the man who is to govern her destiny in life, nor the face of the women with whom she is to reside; cut off from her indulgent mother and the scenes of her childhood, she cannot but feel disgust at the restraints that are imposed upon her in the family circle of her husband. She cannot move about as freely as she was accustomed to do in her father's house, where she was allowed to visit her young companions, and even go into the neighbouring village. She has always to draw the veil over her face, and to hide herself from the view of all the male relations of her husband.

Though living under the same roof with her father-in-law and his sons, she is never permitted to look at any of them for a moment; and if by accident they happen to cross her path, she veils herself as if in the presence of a stranger. Should the mother-in-law be kind-hearted, she will try to comfort the little stranger with sweetmeats or new toys, but her first grief is best soothed by putting her head on the bosom of the nurse who has brought her, and crying herself to sleep—to wake in her prison home, and begin a life of seclusion and inanition.

Of her employments in this new abode, it is difficult to speak—without books or any useful occupation, and without rational intercourse, time hangs heavily on the victim of such a social system. The poorer women must cook and perform family drudgery. In higher circles, where these duties are done by menials, the life of the rich lady is most uninteresting, without diversity or enjoyment. Listening to slander is one of her favourite recreations, and there are always some elderly women attached to a family, usually some widowed relative, whose special business it is to collect and retail gossip for the general amusement. Many a fearful quarrel springing out of such gossip varies the monotony of zenana life.

Usually, however, her day is spent in combing and plaiting the hair, and "putting on of apparel," which, being always alike in its form and fashion, can only be varied by continual change. A lady of rank and wealth counts her garments by hundreds. She is very particular in adorning her person with jewels, which are regarded as pledges of her husband's affection, and she will endure any amount of personal infliction for their sake. She bores her ears in fifty places for her earrings, and her nose for the nose-ring. She never complains of the pricking or weight of the jewels covering her hands, arms, toes, wrists, and ankles, though they can hardly fall short of fifty pounds when she is fully attired.

Personally, a Hindu female is not inferior to those women whom most nations have agreed to adopt for their standard of beauty. Many a lovely and graceful creature adorns the zenana, as the description of one known to the writer will show.

This lady at the time we allude to—sixteen years of age—was small, but well proportioned, with fine features and brilliant eyes. Her *sari*—the one piece of dress for a Bengali female—was most modestly disposed—only a little of her neck, and half way up her arm—which was so far covered with bracelets—could be seen. A gold chain was twisted through her fingers, and then round her arm; and on the back of the hand a large gold medallion, covered with diamonds and rubies, so that but little of it was left uncovered. There was another such ornament on her foot, and a medallion on her instep, beside the anklets.

Her *sari* was of beautiful texture, between gauze and barege, with broad gold border, and must have been of great length, for it was so twisted about her that you could not distinguish her form, and the drapery was graceful and beautiful. Her head was adorned with a comb that looked like a crown of gold, studded with diamonds, rubies, and emeralds, and a gold chain was twisted about her hair with a grand ornament suspended from her forehead. Her nose-ring had three pearls, the centre one very large.*

Such is the outward adornment of a rich Hindu lady, but, alas! neither in childhood or youth is her intellect cultivated, nor does it enter into the mind of her husband to improve her understanding, or raise the tone of her ideas, so as to mould her into a fit companion for his social hours. The little she

* It will interest the reader to be told that the lady whose dress is here described became a believer, and died in the faith of Christ.

may possibly learn is from the young lads of the family, whom she sometimes bribes by presents to give her some instruction, but if she gain it she has access to no books but a few of a puerile and immoral kind.

The virtues of an excellent wife are thus described in the Shastras. Rama thus mourns over the loss of Sita:—"She was not a common wife; in the management of my affairs she ever gave me an excellent counsel; when I needed her service, she was my slave; if I was ever angry, like the patient earth she bore my impatience without a murmur; in the hour of necessity she cherished me as a mother does her child; in the moments of repose she was to me as a charmer; in times of hilarity she was to me as a friend." *

"When engaged in religious services, an excellent wife assists her husband with a mind as devout as his own. On all occasions she gives her whole mind to make him happy, is as faithful to him as a shadow to the body, shares in all his joys and sorrows, and esteems him, whether rich or poor, whether possessed of excellent or evil qualities, whether handsome or deformed. In the absence or sickness of her husband a good wife renounces every gratification, and at his death dies with him."

* See page 18.

CHAPTER IV.

HINDU WOMEN AS WIVES, MOTHERS, AND WIDOWS.

BUT the scene changes. Hindu women, as soon as they become mothers of sons, are important personages in the domestic circle. Their husbands become indulgent towards them, and then treat them with respect; while they, in their turn, begin to exercise a mastery over the actions and conduct of the men. The husband consults his wife on questions of domestic economy, and leaves in her hand all the petty details of household business. Her influence extends even beyond this. As natural guardian of the babe in her arms, the husband gives her all the consideration due to her rank, and suffers himself to be dictated to, not only in respect to domestic affairs, but to his own pursuits in life and mode of conduct.

It is on this account that the Hindus are less adventurous than other nations, and less fitted for innovations in their social system. It is through the influence of women that reformation in India is so effectually opposed in its progress. Young Bengal is full of European ideas when abroad, but quite a Bengali when at home. He eats mutton chops and drinks champagne when in society; within the walls of the zenana, he kneels before the image of stone which is the family idol. Half the amount of education spread over the land would have been sufficient for mighty changes but for their influence.

The attachment of Hindu mothers to their children is inordinate. They keep their little ones always with them, and hear with wonder of English mothers sending their children to England. They call them heartless, for *they* cannot part even with their grown-up sons. A Hindu mother's solicitude for her child is always influencing her. She is the most religious woman in the world, and carefully pours into her new-born infant's mouth the drop of honey prescribed in the Shastras, choosing by the aid of astrology a propitious name, such as Light, Peace, Health, Sweet-scent—all favourites with mothers.

She is all humility and penitence before the gods, that they may preserve her child from sickness, misfortune, and death. She always sends gifts to the Brahmans, and fasts on particular days in the week for the sake of her son, be he but a babe or verging on a good old age. To an Indian mother a son can never grow old, and in return for all this affection she derives no small gratification from the obedience and attachment of her children.

A Bengali child loves its mother far more than its father. Pity that so much affection and tenderness can be turned to no beneficial account through her ignorance. What mother, indeed, has greater opportunities for educating her son and forming his early habits than a Bengali mother, and yet what mother is less capable of doing it aright? As soon as her babe is born she presents it to her god. When it begins to lisp, she teaches it his name; and when it can understand his legends, often diabolical, always depraving, she pours moral poison into the little openings of her babe's soul, until it grows up a confirmed idolater. She recklessly fills the young mind with unworthy ideas, which can with difficulty be eradicated in maturer years. A Bengali's religious sentiments, his belief in the existence of ghosts and evil spirits, his piques and his prejudices, are all owing to the lectures heard by him in the cradle from the lips of a doting mother.

A Bengali woman's attachment for her children is never so severely tried as in the case of a bereavement. Her wailings are pitiable and loud, and her acts such as endanger life. It is indeed bitter grief.

Her distress is also most severe when, under the influence of an enlightened conscience, the children of her own bosom are induced to forsake their homes and their dearest connections for the sake of their spiritual welfare. Her distress is then of the most intense kind, and can only be imagined by one who has seen or felt it. She looks upon such an event as the direst of all calamities; it is to her a cruel bereavement indeed.

But now comes the darkest side of all in this dark picture. There stands behind the scene a modest-looking woman of wretched appearance, though possessed of excellent qualities, the tale of whose life is a tale of pity, for her husband is dead. Yesterday she was blithe and happy, not a cloud was there to frown on her beautiful forehead, and the bloom of youth was on her face. But what a change has come over the spirit of her young dream! The colour has fled from her cheeks, and her loveliness has faded. Her hair is dishevelled, and her garments are of the coarsest kind. Her jewels, which she valued so much in her days of pride, are no longer on her person. Never more must she put them on, never more wear a beautiful dress, or eat other than a given quantity of poor food, and even this not at all twice in every month. Her soul is full of anguish. She seldom mingles, or is allowed to mingle, in the company of her more fortunate sisters, among whom she might once have been the queen of beauty.

She has no longer a share in the festival, for there her presence is a contamination. In the poetical language of her people, she chants between her bursts of tears—"O my beloved, sun of my soul, star of my heart, lord of my affections, why didst thou go away? Did I not make thee happy? Did I not love thee? Was I not always near to comfort thee when thou wast weary? Why then didst thou not stay?" Well may she thus mourn, for from this moment she leads the life of an ascetic and a drudge, be she ever so young.

This picture of a Hindu widow is not imaginary. Her life is one of far greater misery than we can depict. There was a time when many such preferred death to life, and the poor widow abandoned her home and her earthly connections and committed herself to the flames upon the dead body of her husband. This practice, however, has, since the days of Lord William Bentinck, been effectually rooted out of the soil, and numbers have been saved who, according to Hindu usage, were doomed to perish in the flames. But alas for the widow! though her life has been spared, the sentence upon her has been only commuted. The brand is on her brow, and she is doomed for the term of her natural life to sink under the weight of her sorrows.

Happily, we can now add that a Hindu woman is no longer doomed to perpetual widowhood. An Act has been passed by the British Government rendering remarriage lawful; and though custom and prejudice prevent this Act from rapidly taking effect, it is gradually making its power felt in softening the lot of the Hindu widow.

We will conclude our description with a hymn of Krishna, intended for a female worshipper.

"O holy and pure Being, how my heart loves to dwell upon thy attributes! Oh that I were the water in which thou washest thy hands! or the sandal-wood which anoints thy feet! or, oh that I were a garland of red flowers to adorn thy neck for ever! But alas! instead of all this, I am only a woman and a wife.

"I have a jealous mother-in-law, who sends me into the kitchen, and says a woman's sole duty is to cook her husband's food. But, O Krishna! I can think of thee even there; my heart is ever with thee.

"And while my husband's mother thinks it is

the smoke of the kitchen fire that makes my eyes run with water, it is not that, but the remembrance of thy love, O Krishna, that melts my heart and makes it overflow with gratitude."

After reading this sketch, must not the mind of every Christian woman be filled with sympathy when she remembers the insatiable demand of every human soul for variety, and perceives that it can only be furnished to her Hindu sisters by the exercise of their creative imagination. We see this in the hymn we have quoted—the love that wells up in the young heart goes out to Krishna, a wicked and disgustingly immoral God. When a missionary on a preaching tour once noticed a Brahman with a circle of village women round him, to whom he was relating stories of this god's profligate life, the Brahman was so distressed by the missionary's presence, that after coughing and hesitating, he could actually not proceed in his polluting discourse, and twice begged the missionary to leave the place.

Alas! with these women HOPE has no brightening future, FAITH no object to inspire it, AFFECTION no noble or hallowed exercise to raise it above maternal instinct. Even MEMORY, which peoples every other captive's life with the present shadows of the once real past, yields no background of vivid retrospect to relieve the monotony of changeless years for them. *They* cannot be wayside hearers to words that tell of ONE born of woman who came to save their souls, for their feet are fettered. In silent apathy, busy only with their fallen IMAGINA-

TION, they sit, pleading without words, for the visits of their Western sisters to bring them light and life.

Blessed be God, they have not pleaded in vain, and many a Christian worker now shines like a fixed star in the dark night of heathenism, enlightening hearts around her by the tender radiancy of divine truth.

Other chapters will tell the tale of her pupils' progress towards gradually-advancing emancipation, and KNOWLEDGE, MEMORY, and AFFECTION begin to gather round them, filling their hitherto vacant souls with pleasant and precious riches, with a HOPE blooming with immortality, and with FAITH the evidence of things not seen, but believed and enjoyed by anticipation. Well might the women of a zenana, when hearing for the first time a chapter of the Gospel read, involuntarily exclaim, "Surely this book must have been written by a *woman*, for it speaks so kindly of us."

The following letter from a Christian girl betrothed to a young man who died, and addressed to her former teacher, touchingly shows that while the intensely loving heart still writhes under its sorrow, she can turn to a Comforter able to bind up her wound :—

"Oh, if I could but see you, I would throw myself into your arms, and weep, as it were, tears of blood! My eyes are swollen, and my heart is broken ; but 'the Lord gave, and the Lord hath taken away.' He whom I loved and trusted, on whom all my fondest hopes were centred, is gone; but I know who in faithfulness has afflicted me. It is indeed a terrible trial, and I could not leave my bed for two days. My heart rebelled till I remembered, "Himself hath done it," &c., lines sent me by my brother from a Hindu friend who wept with me. 'God hath showed me great and sore troubles, but has quickened me again.' I have indeed experienced the sympathy of my precious Saviour to the fullest extent. The last time we met we had sweet communion together in the 23d and 148th Psalms. It was the depth of his piety I so loved. May I now work for the Lord with whom he is for ever!"

May the life of many a consecrated one among our readers, be led to dedicate its powers to the blessed though trying service of a teacher to the imprisoned women of India in their dark, dull zenanas; and may she reap rich fruit as she watches the springing of the seed she sows, and sees the love of their really tender hearts welling out towards that precious Saviour, who so comforted this poor girl.

CHAPTER V.

HISTORICAL SKETCH OF CHRISTIAN EFFORT ON BEHALF OF HINDU FEMALES.

WE will begin our HISTORICAL SKETCH by a reference to the efforts of the Indian Government for female education.

Though a benevolent, able, and paternal Government, it long abstained from giving direct encouragement to girls' schools, while warmly expressing its desire to see female education extend, and giving indirect aid to Christian and native efforts. At length Lord Lawrence, under the advice and influence of Miss Carpenter, ordered the establishment of State training-schools for girls in Calcutta, Madras, and Bombay, which were by no means successful, and were soon closed, for the plan of a purely secular education has never found real favour with the natives of India. The Government, however, declined to ofund female schools similar to those for boys sustained by the general revenue, perhaps because of the difficulties arising from the peculiar condition of women in India.

Lord Dalhousie was the first to give grants of public money to girls' schools, and to show honour to native gentlemen who founded them. He also sustained the Bethune School from his private purse after the death of the founder, and did all that could be then attempted by the HEAD OF THE SUPREME GOVERNMENT.

The missionaries, ever the pioneers in such attempts, were then only feeling their way in boys' schools, and Government followed.

It might now, twenty-five years later, venture to imitate them again, in the girls' department; but it has not yet acted on this policy, though from time to time expressing its great satisfaction with the advance being made by voluntary workers. A glance at the comparative sums spent on boys' and girls' schools, shows a painfully larger amount disbursed from the public treasury for the former than for the latter.

We make this passing reference to Government action in female education, to show the great importance of missionary effort, and to make manifest the large share it has had in producing what has been effected in India. This is acknowledged in a State paper lately printed, which remarks as follows:—

"The whole subject of missionary enterprise in India has an important bearing on the intellectual advancement of the people. Their efforts on behalf of female education are seen in the zenana schools, and in the classes which are maintained and instructed in the houses of Hindu gentlemen.

"The various lessons which the missionaries inculcate have given to the people at large new ideas; not only on purely religious questions, but on the nature of evil, the obligations of laws, and the motives by which human conduct should be regulated. Insensibly, a higher standard of moral conduct is becoming familiar to the people, especially to the young, which has been set before them, not merely by public teaching, but by the millions of printed books and tracts which are scattered widely through the country.

"They consider that the influences of their religious teaching are assisted and increased by the example of the better portions of the English community, by the spread of English literature and English education, by the freedom given to the press, by the high standard, tone, and purpose of Indian legislation, and by the spirit of freedom, benevolence, and justice which pervades the English rule.

"And they augur well of the future moral progress of the native population of India, from these signs of solid advance gained within the brief period of two generations.

"Without pronouncing an opinion upon the matter, the Government of India cannot but acknowledge the great obligation under which it is laid by the benevolent exertions made by the six hundred missionaries scattered over the country, whose blameless example and self-denying labours are infusing new vigour into the stereotyped life of the great populations placed under English rule, and are preparing them to be in every way better men and better citizens of the great empire in which they dwell."*

We will now proceed to give a brief and informal sketch of the missionary effort which has been made on behalf of female education, and which has brought about the results here acknowledged by the Indian Government, as far as they refer to the female population of their vast empire.

The subject naturally resolves itself into three parts—

I. Early and incipient attempts to form day-schools for the humbler class of girls, the only class at first accessible to missionary effort.

II. The formation of orphanages and free boarding-schools for the daughters of the converts, nearly all of whom were poor people; and,

III. The opening gradually made for entrance into the houses of the higher classes, resulting in what is now commonly spoken of as zenana teaching.

The honour due to the lady who made the earliest effort in the first department must be given to Mrs Hannah Marshman of Serampur, and is referred to in her biography, which will be found at the close of the volume. She attempted a day-school for girls as early as 1807, and in due time her example told on her missionary sisters in Calcutta, Mrs Lawson and Mrs Pearce, wives of Baptist mission-

* These condensed extracts are from the Report of the Secretary of State and Council of India upon THE MORAL AND MATERIAL PROGRESS AND CONDITION OF INDIA. Ordered by the House of Commons to be printed, 28th April 1873.

aries, to whom must be accorded the honour of commencing female education in Calcutta.

In 1819 some young people of East Indian birth, educated and encouraged by these ladies, formed an association called "THE CALCUTTA FEMALE JUVENILE SOCIETY, for the education of native females." They set to work with youthful zeal, and were not discouraged because during the first year the number of their scholars never exceeded eight; at the end of the second year they had thirty-two; and in three years more they numbered six schools and a hundred and sixty pupils.

In December 1821, a year which will ever be memorable in the history of native female education in India (for it was the year of Miss Cooke's arrival), these juvenile workers held the second anniversary of their Society, which was then publicly recognised by the missionary body as an important one.

We will now go back to 1818, in which year was formed THE CALCUTTA SCHOOL SOCIETY, intended to aid in fostering the establishment of schools, and to encourage native gentlemen to attempt to found them spontaneously; for at this time the indigenous Bengali schools only amounted to a hundred and twenty, containing four thousand one hundred and fifty boys, for a population of seven million and fifty thousand natives.

Of girls' schools there were none (the Brahmans and rich men educated *their* sons at home); and out of forty millions of Hindu females which British India then contained (it is much larger now), not one in a hundred thousand could read. This appalling fact induced the Committee, formed of both natives and Europeans, to apply in 1819 to "THE LONDON BRITISH AND FOREIGN SCHOOL SOCIETY," to select and send out a lady to institute schools for native females, and Mr Ward of Serampur, a Baptist missionary then in England, powerfully seconded their request. The advent of Miss Cooke was the result, and in the biography of Mrs M. A. Wilson, it will be seen how happy was the selection made.

The idea was to form a training-school to prepare future teachers, similar to the one which actually came into existence in 1852; but Miss Cooke's ardent mind preferred immediate action, and the providence of God favoured her desires in a striking way.

On the 25th of January 1822, while studying the native language, she visited one of the School Society's boys' schools, to observe their pronunciation. The novel sight of a European lady in that part of the native town caused a crowd to collect, among whom was an interesting-looking little girl, who was driven away. Miss Cooke had her recalled, and by an interpreter asked her if she wished to learn. She was told, in reply, that this child had for three months past been daily begging to be admitted to learn to read among the boys, and that, if she would attend next day, twenty girls should be collected.

Accordingly, on the following morning (26th January), Miss Cooke, accompanied by a friend who could converse familiarly in Bengali, attended, and found thirteen girls assembled. While she was engaged in speaking to them, some of the mothers stood without, looking in through the lattice-work. On Miss Cooke's friend turning towards the latter, they drew their upper coverings over their faces. But not discouraged, she moved towards them, saying, "I hope you will be pleased that your children should be taught; that lady came from Europe solely for the purpose of instructing the children of the natives of this country."

One of them said, "Can she speak our language? Has she been, or is she going to be married?"

The reply was, that "in a short time she would be able to speak their language; that she had heard in England that the women of India were not taught to read or write, and that the men alone were allowed to attain to any degree of knowledge; that she therefore felt much sorrow and compassion for their state, and had determined to leave her country, her parents, her friends, and every other advantage, and come there to educate their daughters."

On hearing this, they with one voice cried out (striking their bosoms with their right hands), "Oh, what a pearl of a woman is this!" It was then added, "She has given up greater expectations to come here, and seeks not the riches of this world, but that she may promote your *best interests.*" "Our children are yours,—we give them to you," replied two or three of the mothers at once.

After a few more questions and answers, they all parted for their respective homes.*

* The reader will perceive, from these details, that poor women are

Two days afterwards, on the 28th, a second visit was paid by Miss Cooke and her friend. They only found seven pupils, among whom were two new faces. Some of the mothers again assembled outside. After a while, one of them asked, "What will be the use of learning to our *girls*, and of what advantage will it be to them?" She was told that "it would enable them to be more useful in their families, increase their knowledge, and gain them respect and affection." "True," said one of them, "our husbands now look upon us as little better than brutes." On which another asked—

"And what benefit will *you* derive from this work?" It was replied, "that the only return wished for, was to promote their best interests and happiness."

"Then," said the woman, "I suppose this is a holy work in your sight, and will be pleasing in the sight of God." To which, as they could not understand the higher Christian motives, it was simply answered that "God is always well pleased that we should come and do good to our fellow-creatures." After some further observations, they parted, the women speaking in terms of the highest approbation of the conduct and replies of the European visitors.

This first attempt at female education having thus unexpectedly commenced in one of the schools of the "School Society," it was the signal for a series of successive institutions. Within a month other two schools were established,—one in a different quarter

not secluded like their richer sisters, but go abroad as occasion requires.

of the town, and another on the Church of England mission premises,—containing in all between fifty and sixty girls.

With unhoped-for rapidity the interest grew. In a few weeks £350 was in hand from benevolent friends, Lord Hastings, then Governor-General, and his wife, heading the subscription. The two schools became ten before the close of the year, and contained two hundred pupils, and this in addition to those of the ladies before referred to.

The strong and unreasonable prejudices of the people were gradually overcome, and by June 1823 a general examination of all the schools showed that many of the girls could actually read some easy books, and do a little needlework. Beyond such incipient attainments it was not then possible to advance, as, on account of early marriages, the girls could seldom remain in attendance over their eighth year. In 1824 the schools having increased to twenty-two, and the pupils to between three and four hundred, a society of European ladies in Calcutta, with the wife of the Governor-General, Lady Amherst, as patroness, formed themselves into a committée, and gave themselves the title of THE LADIES' SOCIETY FOR NATIVE FEMALE EDUCATION in Calcutta and its vicinity; and at an examination which followed in December 1825, the schools were spoken of as thirty in number, and the pupils as four hundred.

From that time, encouraged by the offer of £2000 from a native nobleman, Rajah Boidenath Roy, the erection of a Central building was decided on, the foundation-stone of which was laid by Lady Amherst May 18th, 1826, in the presence of a large and influential assembly.

We will refer our readers to the memoir of Mrs M. A. Wilson for further details, merely remarking that the spell being now broken, and female education publicly allowed to be a possibility—though still confined to the poorest classes—an important victory had been gained, and the friends of missions in other parts of India were not slow to follow the example of Calcutta. None did so at an earlier period, or with more zeal, than Mrs Stevenson, Mrs Margaret Wilson, and their Missionary sisters in Bombay. The result of their efforts is given in a separate chapter.

II. The formation of orphanages and free boarding-schools is the next stage of progress to be noted. The latter were begun by the Baptists, many of whose converts lived in places where European missionaries could not reside. It was to the wife of one of their missionaries, Mrs Ellis, who had such a school in early days, that Mrs Wilson provided a trusty superintendent, a rare woman, who had been converted as a child in her day-school, and had been permitted the joy of leading her father and mother to the Saviour. Similar schools were and still are carried on with much encouragement, not only in Bengal, but in India at large. In the memoir of Mrs Mullens it will be seen how zealously she laboured in this department.

It was Mrs Wilson who conceived the first idea of an orphanage in Bengal, and hers was begun with a few girls who from time to time fell into her hands, and resided with her in the Central school. Enough is said in detail in her Memoir on her particular orphanage, so we will only add that others gradually followed in various parts of India, as at Burdwan, Banares, Cawnpur, Agra, and other places, which were filled to overflowing in those times of periodical floods and famines which deprived such multitudes of Hindu children of their parents and homes. More than half those so collected succumbed to diseases contracted by their sufferings, but enough remained to enable the missionaries to train suitable wives, who became, in many instances, truly converted women, and have formed a goodly band of teachers and matrons for the ever-increasing openings in schools and private residences.

In this and other respects, both orphanages and boarding schools must be regarded as having proved of essential service in the progress of female education and enlightenment.

III. We now come to the third stage of progress, the deep interest in which has been perfectly fascinating, and has aroused the zeal of many hearts, as well as deepened the sympathy and love of Christian ladies at large.

In the memoir of Mary Bird, which tells us of her share in the first efforts of female missionaries, incipient efforts in what is now called zenana visitation are alluded to. We have no record of particular incidents, but may well conclude that her labours in this direction were not in vain, and there seems good reason to hope that, even then, some of these poor immured women learned to look to Jesus, and trust Him, as their Saviour, though the fact was concealed in the depths of zenana seclusion.

But before the arrival of Mary Bird, an attempt to educate Hindu ladies had been made in a village near Calcutta. The opportunity was given by an enlightened gentleman, the son of Babu Jay Narain Ghosal, who presented some valuable property at Banares to the Church Missionary Society, where a college now exists bearing his name.

One of the earlier missionaries (Mr Tracey, of the L. M. S.) was intimate with this gentleman, and often persuaded him to allow his mother, wife, and daughters to be taught. At length he prevailed, because the Babu hoped that if they learned to write, they would tell him their domestic grievances by letter, instead of summoning him home, as they often did, to settle their disputes in person. The missionary's wife was then introduced, and the six ladies became her pupils to their own delight and hers, for they received instruction eagerly and intelligently.

But friends remonstrated, and the poor Babu felt constrained to stop progress, by politely informing the teacher that his family were going to visit his father at Banares—a mere excuse, as they never left home. About two years after, the lady teacher gained permission to visit her old pupils, who received her enthusiastically, inquiring why she had so long forsaken them; and when she told them, they were deeply grieved, having been kept in entire ignorance of the fact. They then besought the Babu to permit her to return, which he did, and their education was continued. This is the first attempt we can trace of a missionary teacher gaining access to a zenana.

Some years later Mrs Wilson was admitted to visit, and instruct in English, the wife of Rajah Boidenath Roy, and when the Central school, erected chiefly through his munificence, came into active operation, his Rani wished to visit it, and consented to meet a party of English ladies who assembled to receive her there. She was extremely delighted, and made a most pleasing impression on all present.

CHAPTER VI.

PROGRESS OF ZENANA VISITATION.

We now pass over several years, during which many ardent desires were felt, and many earnest prayers ascended from loving womanly hearts for their imprisoned sisters.

Whispers came across the great Indian continent, that the Parsis of Bombay had summoned an English teacher to commence the education of their women, as early as 1842, and hopes rose and fell by turns. Here and there some humble maid servant of low caste would reveal to a missionary's wife that she was privately teaching her mistresses to read, from books she had received in the missionary day school; and then a native gentleman would be met by the way, and would earnestly remark, "Madam, our wives must have knowledge; we see they must; but how is it to be conveyed to them?" and she would find that light was surely though secretly penetrating zenana walls.

In 1849-50, a benevolent Scotchman made a courageous attempt at his own expense, to open a school for the better class of girls in Calcutta. He erected a house, and designated it "The Bethune Institution."

He provided closed conveyances to bring the girls to and from school, and paid the lady superintendent a handsome salary. He tried to allure the Hindus by promising that no Christianity should be taught, though he gratefully availed himself of the willingness of a Christian missionary's widow to take charge of the establishment, which she did in the hope that she might privately find opportunities, out of school hours, to commend Christ to the acceptance of some with whom she might be brought into contact through her position. Doubtless many a good impression has been thus made. Yet, as a whole, this really noble effort strikes one as simply a costly failure; the rich but not the high born girls have been influenced to attend, and it has been seen in this, as it was in other cases where Christianity was ignored, that no real blessing rested on the attempt.

Far different was the result when Dr Duff inaugurated a high caste girls' school on a more natural, simple, and ingenious plan, for this has proved a decided success.

It is indeed chiefly attributable to the clear insight of *his* master mind, that we may trace the opening of the Hindu zenana. He saw, on his arrival in India in 1832, that to gain access to the women we must first, by educating and influencing the views of the men, awaken the Hindu mind from the sleep of ages; and he patiently set to work to accomplish this. He has lived to witness the result and to rejoice over it with the present labourers.

Soon after the establishment of "THE BETHUNE

INSTITUTION" in 1850, an event occurred of thrilling interest. The highly educated son of an influential Hindu gentleman, living in a princely mansion, had privately instructed his gifted and beautiful young wife, with whom he read among other books the English Bible. He was under promise to his mother never to become a Christian; but he read the Scriptures because they were interesting as an historical study.

The entrance of the Word gave light to the heart of that young wife, and she besought her husband to accept Christ as his Saviour. A widowed cousin of fourteen read with them, and she also believed, but the husband resisted. The young wife sickened and died,—died trusting in Jesus for salvation,—the husband's heart yielded; he was baptized; and the cousin, as soon as circumstances permitted, followed his example, and has long been the wife of a native Christian convert.

These conversions made a deep impression on Christian hearts, and, combined with other circumstances, led to effective effort, which took the form of founding an institution for training the daughters of European and East Indian parents born in India, and familiar with the language. It was believed that such teachers for Hindu ladies would ere long be needed, though at the time they were still inaccessible. Such an institution, it will be remembered, had been projected but not initiated in 1820, when Miss Cooke was invited to come out for the purpose of conducting it. A lady superintendent was now again sent for from England, and this time the plan took effect, and "THE CALCUTTA NORMAL SCHOOL" became, from February 1852, a fixed institution of that city.

Instead of one lady two sisters entered on the work, who were admirably suited to give a high tone to its initiatory attempt, and this high tone it has ever retained.

The very first of its trained teachers was engaged by the Rev. John Fordyce, superintendent of "The Free Church of Scotland Missionary Boarding School," in 1853. His sympathies were all alive for the enthralled Hindu ladies, and he printed a series of fly-leaves which were widely circulated throughout India. They contained short, strong, and striking appeals to Hindu husbands and fathers, and produced an impression which deepened year by year, so that at first one by one, and afterwards in increasing ratio, zenana doors flew open, till at this moment the question is not, How shall we get in? but, How shall we supply labourers for the much work ready to be done?

All honour to the Christian love and zeal, the really chivalrous attempt of our beloved brother, the Rev. John Fordyce.

Such were the initiatory steps in the laying of the foundation-stone of the beautiful and stately temple, into which we believe the naturally highly-gifted ladies of India are destined to grow.

We must now touch on one or two collateral circumstances tending to aid in the result at which Mr Fordyce arrived.

In 1856, an enlightened though not a Christian native doctor, a great favourite with Mrs Mullens, died, leaving a widowed household, so singularly helpless that, finding she could read, Mrs Mullens induced his intelligent daughter to open a private girls' school in her own house. This was called a zenana school, and it succeeded well, numbering soon twenty-three good class girls; seventeen children, six wives and mothers. It took the place of a common day-school Mrs Mullens had carried on before, and was far more satisfactory; for the widow was indefatigable, and soon became an enthusiast in her vocation. Mrs Mullens herself gave some hours every week to impart Christian instruction.

In May 1857, an opportunity opened for Dr Duff to make a somewhat similar attempt on the other side of the city, and close to his boys' institution. An intelligent Kulin Brahman (in spite of his rank) consented to let two rooms of his own house to the Doctor for a female school, and to use his influence in obtaining Brahman pupils, and another Kulin volunteered to send a few from his neighbourhood.

On the opening day three appeared, and a few days later ten were counted, Dr Duff giving daily attendance to encourage the incipient experiment.

The ages of these quick, intelligent, engaging little maidens varied from five to nine. They progressed rapidly, and as soon as they could read were shown a map of India, and made to understand the relative position of places, and form some idea of the size of their country. As their eyes wandered from north to south, it seemed as if a new sun had burst before them on a new world; their delight was unbounded; but when the Doctor told them he had traversed Ceylon, popularly believed to be peopled by giants, they evidently questioned his veracity, as they were sure no one who had been there could return alive.

On hearing that he had seen the sacred walls and temples of their holy city Banares, he was affected by their grasping his hand, saying they "could not help touching one who had been there." Yet they received with infantile simplicity his assurance that there was only one great God.

But when twenty of these promising pupils were seen clustering around him on his daily visit, a malicious Kulin came forward, and almost ruined the whole affair. The good Doctor, however, persevered, and weathered the storm; the work rallied; and a few weeks later above forty girls of the highest caste (although many of them poor, for Hindu noblemen, though they never lose their honourable or high position, are often destitute of wealth) were in daily attendance.

Both Mrs Mullens and Dr Duff had adopted inexpensive though effectual plans for meeting the native prejudice against allowing girls to pass public streets unguarded, and this aided and greatly accounted for the success of their experiment. Both were also singularly favoured in the very efficient mistresses they obtained, and both bestowed in the beginning much personal attention to the pupils.

Passing over the rapid openings of 1861, during which Mrs Mullens, a host in herself, was permitted to labour in zenanas, we go on to relate that in 1862, a committee of ladies in London, originally formed to co-operate with the Calcutta ladies, sent out their first zenana missionary, and, in the same year, Miss Brittain arrived from America. Their objects were identical and threefold, as we have mentioned in another chapter. Miss B.'s success has also been alluded to in the same chapter.

That of "THE INDIAN NORMAL SCHOOL AND INSTRUCTION SOCIETY," for such was the name given to the English association, has been equally marked; so that now, from Trevandrum, the capital of the native kingdom of Travancore, on the south-west, to Umritser, the sacred city of the Sikhs, on the north,—taking in on the route, Madras, Masulipatam, Calcutta, Lucknow, Banares, Lahore, Jullundur, &c., besides Bombay on the west,—their female missionaries are located.

As this society has been formed for India alone, it is able to concentrate all its power there, and its operations are widening year by year.

It will be impossible to allude to all the stations in detail, but we will say a few words about each.

Trevandrum was entered on at the invitation of the Prime Minister of the reigning Prince, a most enlightened and highly-educated Hindu gentleman, who prevailed on the Rajah to permit the education of the Ranis, and other ladies of the royal household. His invitation was backed by the British Resident at the court, a Christian gentleman, deeply interested in the enlightenment of Hindu women, and was responded to by a lady singularly qualified to enter on the work. Her patient perseverance—for here, as elsewhere, much prejudice had to be overcome, notwithstanding the high patronage—has been rewarded with success, and she can now tell of sixty-eight girls in her Malayalim school, and a Prince presiding at its annual examination: of a goodly number in her English school, held in a room given by the Rajah, and attended by girls of position and most pleasing appearance, with deep love for their teacher.

At *their* annual examination the Maharajah was present in person, with his staff, and he distributed the prizes. The number of the private lady pupils steadily increases; they are the wives, mothers, sisters, and daughters of the reigning Sovereign and his Princely relatives; several of them most lovely and interesting women, full of politeness and cordiality to their missionary teacher, who is regarded by them as a trusted friend and adviser.

We now make a long journey across the peninsula to Madras on the Coromandel coast, where a native lady and her daughters are indefatigable in their labours.

The Madras Presidency is in advance of the others as a whole, for it became the scene of missionary labours many years before either Calcutta or Bombay. We cannot here give even a sketch of what is doing in female education in the various missionary stations scattered over its area, and must confine our remarks to Masulipatam, lying higher up on the coast.

Here the lengthened labours of Mr Noble (whose missionary aims resembled those of Dr Duff) have told on the male population, and prepared a warm welcome for zenana teachers. Striking and touching conversions have occurred, and, though Mr Noble was not favoured as Dr Duff is, to live to witness his ardent aspirations realised, they are being fulfilled, to the joy of those who have succeeded him.

Here English teachers are now located, ready to enter any zenanas that may open, and some have opened already. The wife of a missionary, who for five years conducted and still carries on, though now a widow, a large girls' day school, has helped to clear the way, by overcoming prejudices, and preparing native teachers as auxiliaries to the zenana missionary.

Other girls' schools also exist, and of no station do we read more thrilling and romantic stories of the efforts made by converted young men to recover their wives, than of this. Some of these rescued women are now mistresses of girls' schools, proving admirable, zealous, and successful teachers.

We now cross the Bay of Bengal, and enter the sacred river of the Hindus, the holy Ganges, at its mouth, making our way up one branch of the stream, the Hughli, till we land at Calcutta—bound to Englishmen by so many strong and social ties. The European quarter, with its thirty thousand inhabitants, its palatial residences, its cathedral, its numerous churches, and its crowded port, is known to almost every one.

The dark regions beyond, where in their lordly mansions the wealthy native gentry still maintain their social and domestic institutions, surrounded by a vast dependent population of all ranks, numbering about 700,000 souls, is comparatively hidden from view. But it is to the female inmates of these secluded homes, that the sympathetic interest of the approaching zenana missionary goes forth. It is in this city that so much concentrated effort has been spent, and it has told, for it is now a fact that its intelligent sons are strongly influencing the whole of North India.

The thorough education of the Bengali gentleman makes him a necessity in those upper provinces where the Government of India largely employs native officers, and he removes with his entire family to distant places, where he and his fellow-citizens congregate in colonies, usually called the Bengali quarter. The zenana missionary follows them, and finds a welcome among them in their distant homes.

It will be seen from the Memoir of Miss Gomez, that not simply at Calcutta, but at adjacent places, as Thakarpukar, Howrah, Barrackpur, &c., the openings are numerous and blessed with the highest kind of success, the true conversion of Hindu ladies. To our chapter on the Zenana and its Inmates, we must refer our readers for details, and pass on to Lucknow, the capital of the Mussulman kingdom of Oude, and morally the lowest in India.

Although but recently occupied, great encouragement has been given to the agents of each society represented here. At first it took effect on the Bengalis exclusively, but all at once, when a temporary check came from that quarter, Mohammedan houses, hitherto far more prejudiced than Hindu, unexpectedly opened their doors, and a wonderfully adapted native teacher arrived at the moment, prepared to enter in.

This was a dear old native Christian lady, who had been baptized a few months before, after years of patient study of God's Word without any human teacher. She was full of zeal and love to her Saviour, and her heart burned to tell the glad tidings of His grace to her people. She is an Arabian by birth, but naturalised in India, by marriage to a Hindu Mussulman, and well acquainted with the Koran in Arabic and other religious books, which she studied in her youth. Most beautifully does she set before her sisters the "old, old story" of the Saviour's love. She neither courts nor shuns controversy. She is well prepared to enter on it, when needed, but soon manages to turn again to her favourite theme, the love and grace of Christ, and she has already won many a jewel for His crown.

Such are the beginnings of success in this wicked city—many miles in extent, with 300,000 souls to be taught of three distinct classes—Bengali, Mohammedan, and Hindu. One of these Mohammedan ladies lately said to her teacher, "I believe in the

God of the Bible and in Him only, but if my husband knew me to be a Christian he would turn me into the street."

We now journey on to Banares, the stronghold of Hinduism, and regarded by the Hindus as so holy, that the greatest sinner dying within ten miles of its precincts, will pass into the highest heaven.

Persevering labours in common girls' schools have been for many years, and are still carried on here, as well as schools for Christian and orphan girls, several of whom have formed materials for a well-conducted training school. Thus here, as elsewhere, the zenana teacher from Europe is provided with an efficient staff, both of those prepared on the spot, and those sent from "The Calcutta Normal School." Vigour and life are marked features in the work at Banares, and rapid progress is manifest, both in zenana visitation and zenana schools. There is a large Bengali colony in the city, and the usual success among this class, some of which is of the kind our hearts long for— the drawing of precious souls to the Saviour.

But we must not linger here, and pass on to Jullundur, where the daughters of a native pastor are the workers, and from thence to Lahore the capital of the Punjaub, where the zenana missionary has six schools, containing several hundred pupils. In each of these she perceives signs of encouraging progress, and in unexpected quarters has work been found for willing hands, while many a new field has opened for cultivation. She has also more zenanas than she is able to visit, and what is best, she has gathered some first-fruits from both departments.

One of her refreshments has been to pay visits to a Bengali Christian lady, intercourse and communion with whom has strengthened her faith, showing her what Jesus can do by His Spirit for the guidance and teaching of His lonely ones. This lady was converted by reading a Bible with her husband, who at length permitted her to be baptized, though his own heart remained hardened. He however continues to live with her, and so blameless is her conduct, so irreproachable her life, that he allows her to keep her sons with her, though often cruelly oppressive in his behaviour towards her. Her elder son of fifteen was very bitter, but her tender motherly love has softened him, and the younger of twelve declares that he is a Christian like herself.

A Hindu gentleman, a friend of her husband, who never saw her, was helped to decide on professing Christ, by hearing of her excellencies, and a recent female convert, a Sikh woman, found in her a sister and a friend. For a long time she kept strictly secluded according to her husband's desire, but he was induced by the zenana missionary to let her come to the Lord's Supper, and then to the Sunday morning service in the native church, where she shone with a bright and steady light.*

An important addition to the work at Lahore, is a school recently commenced for the daughters of

* Later tidings from this lady lead us to fear she has been subjected to very cruel treatment from her nearest connections. She is no longer at Lahore.

native Christians, in the hope of preparing a staff of indigenous teachers for the work so rapidly opening on all sides.

Having now completed the circle, we take leave of our readers at the sacred city of Umritser, the religious capital of the Punjaub, where two of our lady missionaries have begun to labour among Sikh women, on the usual plan, and from whom we already hear words of cheer, impelling us to go forward in the name of the Lord, till we take possession of India's long-oppressed daughters for Christ.

We must not close our notices without a line in reference to a most excellent Normal School at Ludiana (from whence came the call to world-wide prayer in 1859–60),—commenced, and most efficiently conducted, by an agent of the Society for Promoting Female Education.

Our history would be incomplete were we to omit a word on the subject of Bible-women, whose work we recognise as a very important branch of the efforts being made for Hindu women.

These dear, humble Christian sisters, are the sowers going out to the highways and hedges, the streets and lanes of the city, up and down in all sorts of out-of-the-way places, depositing that incorruptible seed which cannot fail in due time to spring up and bring forth fruit. Many of them possess deep personal piety and ardent Christian love. They need both, to sustain them in their gentle, unobtrusive work, which, though not yet showing immediate results, will by and by be found to have made the first impression upon many a poor wanderer among the maimed, the halt, and the blind, who shall one day press into the kingdom before some of their more favoured people. Bible-women are now scattered all over India, and their journals manifest a remarkable adaptability for their special work.*

* We have not introduced any notice of the valuable labours of American ladies here, but it will be seen in Chapter XX. how extensive and blessed they are. "The London Bible and Domestic Missions" are also represented in India. We see touching sketches, from time to time, of one and another there connected with this "Missing Link" in its monthly magazine.

CHAPTER VII.

SKETCH OF FEMALE EDUCATION IN BOMBAY, OR WESTERN INDIA.

It was in Calcutta, as we have seen, that the first vigorous attempt was made, more than half a century ago, to educate the females of India. Bombay stands next in order of time, and it will be evident, from the Memoirs of Mrs Margaret Wilson, that the foundation was laid there not only wisely and zealously, but very effectively.

We may refer our readers to her Memoir for such notices of these initiatory efforts as are interwoven with Mrs Wilson's personal history, and only remark here very briefly, that it was about the year 1828 that Mrs Stevenson, the wife of a missionary from Scotland, then labouring in Bombay, made the first attempt to gather together little girls of the humbler classes, and to influence their mothers. She was so far successful that, on Mrs Wilson's arrival in 1829, four small schools—bazaar schools, as they are called—were in operation, which, under her fostering care, soon increased in numbers and efficiency. Mrs Stevenson had meanwhile removed to Puna, in the interior, and continued her labours there; while in Bombay the work went steadily forward, so that at the time of Mrs Wilson's death in 1845, the children were counted in these bazaar schools by hundreds.

At this distance of time we can but indistinctly trace the effect produced by these incipient efforts. That they had their influence in helping to undermine prejudice, as well as in cases of individual conversion, we cannot but believe; but that these effects were not commensurate with the labour and expense they cost is evident.

But in reference to the Orphan and Boarding School (alluded to in Mrs Wilson's Memoir), which was founded some years subsequently, and to the institution for educating girls of better position in a superior manner, commenced at a still later period, we can tell of delightful results; for labourers now in the field are reaping good fruit from the seed sown in tears by those who have entered into their rest.

Many of those trained in the mission-schools, especially of those educated in the Female Orphanage, are now actively and successfully engaged in mission-work.

Owing partly to the greater freedom allowed to Mahratta women, as compared to women in other parts of India, and partly to the energetic and independent spirit of the Mahratta people, there are not a few native Christian women in Western India, both married and single, who take a prominent place among Christian workers, while they also gain the respect of the native community generally. The names of Mrs Narayan Sheshadri, Saguna bai Mazda, Saguna bai Haripant, and of many others, are becoming as familiar among the friends of missions at home as they are already throughout the Presidency of Bombay.

To give our readers a more lively idea of such women as are here alluded to, we have added to our biographical notices some letters addressed by one of them who laboured many years as a single woman to an English friend. It would be very delightful to gather together in minute detail the cases of these once degraded daughters of India, now daughters of the Lord Almighty, serving Him in all humility, and adorning the doctrine of their God and Saviour in this and other parts of India; but this cannot be done here.

These examples of Christian training have convinced the so-called Hindu reformers of Bombay that female education means something more than learning to read, write, and sew, and have led them to admit the evil tendency of early marriages, the degradation of widows, and other injurious practices. We believe that practical results will gradually follow, and that in due time the remarriage of widows will not be a rare occurrence.

The Parsis were the first among the natives of Western India to move independently in the matter of female education, and they have carried it on to a greater extent than any others. In a report published a few years ago, Dr Wilson mentions the pleasure he had in finding that Parsi girls, to the number of a thousand, were receiving education in the schools connected with the single institution of Sir Jamsetji Jejibhai.

The recent origin of this movement, as compared with the effort of missionaries in the same direction, appears at once when we consider that the first Parsi girls' schools were opened in 1849, whereas the missionary-schools had begun in 1828. In 1862 we find that more had been done by the people themselves for female education in Bombay than in any other part of India. This has arisen *mainly* from the predominance of the Parsis, who are unshackled by the trammels of *caste*.

In some cases the girls in their schools are educated in English, and taught very much as in an English school. In other cases, and for the most part, the education is vernacular, and the ordinary habits of native life are not interfered with. At the annual examination of these schools, when the prizes are distributed, it is especially interesting and gratifying to observe the evident marks of social respectability in the gay throng of children who assemble. The Hindu and Parsi gentlemen who take part in the proceedings, and who in some instances prove their zeal in the cause by great personal exertion, and the expenditure of both time and money, are men of high character and position in the community.

If this initiatory movement in the work of female education in Bombay had had no other effect than that of directing attention to the manifold evils in the condition of Hindu women, its importance could hardly be over-estimated.

The late Mrs Isabella Wilson* and Mrs Nesbit (now Mrs Anderson) were among the first to engage in the work of visiting native ladies in their homes in Bombay.† The essential requisite for this, as for all mission-work in Western India, is a knowledge of the vernacular; and every missionary will join in the prayer for a greater number of ladies who shall be willing to qualify themselves for this work by taking the trouble to acquire the language.

Alas! that generation after generation of English women have left the shores of India without having attempted to aid in raising those of their own sex among whom their best and brightest years have been passed. Happily there are a few who not only adorn the doctrine of God their Saviour, but who seek the good of those around them, and make known the Gospel to such as are yet strangers to it; and if the number of these aggressive Christians is small, their influence for good extends far and wide.

But especially do we rejoice in the fact, that there are now in Western India many native Christian women, members of native Christian families, employed in seeking to spread abroad throughout their native land the privileges and advantages which have been bestowed on themselves.

* Second wife of Dr Wilson, the husband of Mrs Margaret Wilson.

† Our chapter on "The Zenana and its Inmates" contains some graphic notices of this branch of work in Bombay.

They can speak with peculiar emphasis of the benefits of Christian education, for they can quote their own experience as an example of the effect of an acquaintance with Christian truth in producing emancipation from the thraldom of superstition and evil habits. They can tell how they have been brought out of darkness into light, and have been introduced into a society where the only bond is that of a common sympathy and a common hope. They can tell that though they have broken the fetters of caste, they are not without the restraint and obligations of social relationships, but that it is their delight and their privilege to acknowledge those obligations, and to perform all those social duties.

They can tell how they find in the Word of God, which has become the rule of their life, not only the warrant for their new position, but plain, suitable directions for a life and conversation corresponding to the advantages they now enjoy. They can explain that though the word *family* has a different meaning for them as Christians from that which it had for them as Hindus, and though a Christian wife and mother occupies, in virtue of these very relationships, a more independent and responsible position than would be assigned to her in a Hindu household, this independence and responsibility are valued only as enabling her more efficiently to discharge her new duties; and instead of being an occasion for indulgence, lead rather to a more constant exercise of self-denial, and to the cultivation of that meek and quiet spirit which is in the sight of God of great price.

CHAPTER VIII.

SKETCH OF FEMALE EDUCATION IN THE MADRAS PRESIDENCY.

We have passed over Madras in our history, but so many events of deep interest have occurred there, that we must give a brief notice of them in a separate chapter.

The Society for Promoting Female Education has done much in this Presidency, and without referring to earlier efforts made by the older missionaries, before its establishment, we go on to speak of the valuable aid it has rendered to missionaries' wives, in enabling them to found village schools, which have been eminently useful in their own localities.

It is to this Society we are indebted for the great efficiency of the much-blessed girls' day-school in Masulipatam; and still higher up the coast, in Orissa, there are traces in all the missionary-stations of the labours of its agents.* It would be pleasant to tarry here, for it is in the orphan schools at Cuttack, the capital, that we find the dear Khund children rescued from

* The celebrated Juggernath festival is held at Puri, in this district, where congregate tens of thousands of pilgrims from all parts of India.

the bloody Meriah sacrifice by the British Government, and placed by its agent in the care of the missionaries for Christian training. Most richly have many of these little ones repaid in their useful lives the love of those who received them, by becoming valuable fellow-helpers.*

Leaving Cuttack, we return to the south, where, in consequence of the numerous conversions, large bodies of Christian children have to be educated. Many of these showing special abilities for teaching, a training-school was founded in Tinnevelly, called the SARAH TUCKER INSTITUTION, in remembrance of a lady who did much for South Indian female missions. This has yielded valuable fruit, in producing intelligent Christian teachers for those districts. We cannot go on to particularise, or attempt even to name the various stations, where a good deal has been effected for the education of the women, but advancing to Madras itself, we must allude to its greatest benefactress, Mrs Margaret Anderson.

* To those who have not heard of the Meriah sacrifices, we may explain, that in the Khund district, which is adjacent to Cuttack, it has from time immemorial been the custom to fatten children for sacrifice to the Goddess of Agriculture.

The finest boys and girls are selected, and are well fed and brought up in every indulgence till the appointed day, when the annual assembly collects, and the various cultivators attend, with sharpened knives. The children, to the number of fifty or more, are placed in a central spot, and the men fall upon them, cutting pieces out of their tender flesh, till they are stripped bare. With these pieces, reeking in blood, they hasten to their fields, and plant the offering, which ensures a crop at the next harvest. This dreadful custom being now suppressed, the people take a lamb instead of a child, praying most devoutly that the goddess will forgive them for the substitution.

In this city, as in Calcutta, Bombay, and at Masulipatam, it is to the indefatigable labours of the SCOTTISH MISSIONARIES on behalf of the men, that we must trace the opening made for approach to the women.

Mrs Anderson, the wife of one of these missionaries, and personally gifted with singular devotedness and ability for her work, permitted also an unusually long sphere of service in it, stands out prominently before us as the spiritual mother of several of the best and most useful native Christian women in Madras; the general impression made on the native community by her long and devoted course is shown by their expressed appreciation of her.

In an address presented to her by them in 1859, they allude to her, not only with deep respect and admiration, but with warm affection. They speak of her noiseless energy, of her enduring patience and firmness, coupled with extreme tenderness—qualities called into exercise, and exemplified in her training of girls, at one time five together, who forsook their homes and families for Christ's sake, and found shelter and motherly love under her fostering care.

Ten day-schools for respectable girls, containing more than seven hundred, besides a boarding-school, added to the work alluded to under her own roof, give us some idea of Mrs Anderson's labours even as far back as 1859. Blessed be God, she still lives to carry them on;—since 1854 as a widow.

Another dear labourer, who worked hand in hand

with Mrs Anderson, Mrs W. Porter, was similarly blessed during her comparatively few years of missionary labour.

Passing over the intervening period, we come to 1872, and find the wife and daughters of a native pastor in full work at Madras, both in zenana visitation and girls' schools. Mrs Sattianadan often gives details of touching interest in her letters, in reference to each of these spheres; we must only add one brief extract:—"My daughter Annie holds prayer-meetings for children every week, and collects money for the missionary-box. Each child prays in her turn; and one, who is much troubled about her heathen mother, always remembers her in words like these, 'Heavenly Father, when wilt Thou receive my mother into Thy fold?' It touches us to hear her fervent and simple petitions. May the Lord answer them. These little ones have, during the last six months, collected more than eight shillings for the missionary-box."

Mrs Sattianadan adds—"I have five girls' schools with three hundred children, and thirty zenanas with forty ladies, on my hands, so they are full; and I often cry out, 'Who is sufficient for these things?'"

Other agencies are at work in Madras of a similar kind; but with the mention of these we will close, as they convey a lively idea of the great amount of work being done among the women, and of the blessing that accompanies the labourers.

CHAPTER IX.

THE ZENANA AND ITS INMATES.

WHAT is a zenana? This is a question constantly asked by those who are being aroused to sympathy for their Hindu sisters; and it may be briefly answered, that it is literally "The place for women," from the Persian word "zen," a woman, and "ana," place; but this is not all it means and implies.

"A native house," writes a Hindu gentleman, "has generally two divisions, namely, the outer and the inner apartments. The former occupy the greater space of the two, consisting of sitting and reception rooms, exclusively for the male members of the household; a hall, or *dalan*, for the celebration of pujas and festivals; and an open courtyard, for nautches* and other entertainments. These apartments are more or less commodious, and more or less airy, according to the means, taste, and inclinations of the owner of the household.

"Further on, and at the back of the dalan, are the inner apartments, the *untuppoor*, or the zenana, into which are consigned the females of a Bengali house-

* Dances.

hold, our mothers and our wives, our daughters and our sisters—in fact, all the dearest partners and associates of our social existence. The construction of these apartments is always the subject of jealous scrupulousness.

"There must be as few windows as possible, and where they cannot be altogether avoided, care is taken that they do not open on a public street, or on a neighbour's house; and they evidently try to keep out the sunshine and the wind of heaven as much as possible."

Another says—"The zenana is that part of the house of a native gentleman in which the women live, entirely distinct from that occupied by the men, and usually presenting to the eye of the European the appearance of a prison; for the windows, if any, on the outside, are very small and high up, so as effectually to preclude the possibility of the women looking out, or of any one from the outside looking in.

"The houses of the upper classes of the Hindus in Bengal are often large; for sons, when they marry, do not set up a house of their own, as in England, but bring their wives to their father's house, in which they all live together, and the younger woman becomes subject to the elder, and all to the mother-in-law. Often three or four generations are thus living in the same house."

And yet another writes—"Up to this time our women have been the most miserable drudges on the face of the earth; 'cribbed, cabined, and confined' within the four walls of their prison-house, all their curiosity is nipped in the bud, all enjoyments are proscribed to them."

And to turn from native testimony to a missionary's sketch, we add—" Hindu ladies spend their lives in the interior of the zenana or women's apartments. Very early marriage often commits a little girl of five years to the wholly unsympathetic companionship of a man of fifty, sixty, or eighty; married life to her means little more than sorrowful submission to the tyranny of a step-mother and the amusement of a husband, who, if he be kind, treats her as a toy; and when he dies, she enters on a widowhood in which the fires, which, if British law had not forbidden it, would have consumed her with the corpse of her husband, are transmuted into the lingering woe of a social penal servitude, only to terminate with death.

" Bereft of ornaments, her long black tresses shorn off, clothed in the commonest apparel, spending two days in every month without food or water, her employments little more than the meaningless routine of Hindu worship, unconsoling, uninteresting, uninstructive; the childless widow, herself perhaps a child, drinks to its dregs the bitterest cup of a soulless heathenism, whose only law is fate.

" Doubtless there are bright and happy exceptions, but they are *not* the fruits of the system. Doubtless the advance of civilisation and enlightenment is already thundering at the doors of this cruel captivity; but an unsanctified freedom to these poor suffering sisters will be hardly a happier lot. We want Christian women to teach them the glad tidings of great joy, to illumine with gospel light these cheerless homes, and to create, with God's blessing, a freedom of faith which shall anticipate all other enfranchisement, and an obedience of faith which will control and sanctify liberty."

But now we must take our friends *inside* some of those zenanas, and introduce them to a few of the pupils taught by our lady missionaries, and we shall choose examples from the very beginning of the work.

In October 1859 Mrs Wylie writes—"Shortly after I wrote to you last, I spent a very interesting afternoon in visiting the zenanas, in company with Miss Cockle, the lady superintendent of the Normal School, and Mrs Gourley, assistant teacher, and the native girl who accompanies her. It was very affecting to see the poor women and their children, so thankful for the least instruction given them, so eager for the visits of their teachers. The same ground must be gone over day after day, the A B C work, carried on under a tropical sun, in the midst of foul ditches, open sewers, and defective drains, and surrounded by a moral degradation still greater, if possible, than anything that the Bible-women encounter in St Giles's or Whitechapel, and this too amongst the more respectable class, whose husbands are educated men, employed as clerks in the different offices.

"You can scarcely picture to yourself anything more miserable than their homes · small tenements of two stories, built round a very small courtyard, into which no ray of sun penetrates. The long dank grass and weeds grow up in profusion round a deep well in the centre. The house has all the appearance of a ruin, brick and plaster falling out; and here they are pent up in small confined rooms, or sitting in a small outer gallery running round this courtyard, unknown and uncared for, and with no light or ray of truth to cheer or purify, or to reveal that God who died to save them."

At a later date we read—"To-day I went with Miss Nicholson to a large native house, where four ladies were taught and two children. To reach the apartment in which the lessons were given, we mounted a steep brick staircase, which led us to the roof of the house, across which we walked, and found some very secluded rooms set apart for the ladies and their children.

"These ladies were all well advanced, and seemed to enjoy being taught. They learned arithmetic, to which the Burra-bow* and a young widow seemed to be very partial. The Burra-bow worked beautifully in wool-work, and showed me many mats and comforters she had made. As a rule, I may observe the Bengali ladies are very fond of wool-work, and often exhibit great taste in the disposition of colours. They make slippers, and are delighted to work smoking-caps for their husbands and fathers. They pay for their own materials, and many a leisure hour is now spent by these ladies in wool-work which,

* Chief wife.

but for this new acquirement, would be wasted in gossip.

"At this house; near the apartment in which we sat, I observed several pots of flowers and shrubs, the pets of the widow, and her peculiar care. There was no access to a garden, so the natural love of flowers could only be gratified by the possession of these pots on the roof.

"I liked greatly the little peep I had of these ladies; they appeared affectionate towards each other, and the children of one seemed to be the children of all the others. The room was small, but neat and clean, furnished with a wardrobe for their clothes, the precious wool-box, and a tuktaposh, which means a great square wooden stool, almost like a bedstead, excepting that it is scarcely two feet from the ground. It seems very often to take the place of chairs in Bengali houses. I have frequently been to houses where there were no chairs, but always a tuktaposh, on which we were invited to sit. In this house two of the bows squatted crosslegged upon it, and went through their lessons very methodically and laboriously during the two hours of Miss Nicholson's visit.

"On our leaving them, they begged me to come again soon to see them, and accompanied us to the top of their brick staircase, the boundary of their quarter of the house."

Again—"I visited a zenana, consisting of one small room, no windows for ventilation; yet the place was not devoid of comfort, there being a bed in the corner, and two chairs! The wife was the only pupil here, rather an interesting young woman of about twenty years of age. She possessed the New Testament, from which she slowly made out part of a chapter of St Matthew's Gospel in Bengali. The husband is a clerk in a railway office.

"We then set forth to a very ruined house, down a filthy lane, at the head of which we left our conveyance, and proceeded on foot. Here there were six ladies under instruction. The room in which we sat was on the ground floor, small, very damp, and had a close smell. The ladies squatted on the big tuktaposh, leaning against the long bolsters, with their books and slates resting on their knees. They are of a respectable family, though apparently not very rich."

Again we read—"Here there are six pupils, four women and two little girls. One of the women is a great invalid, so does not learn very often. The other day I went to see her in her own room; she was lying on a hard wooden bedstead, *without a mattress*, prostrate with fever. She could scarcely speak to me; but I tried to say a few words of affectionate sympathy, and pointed her to the precious love of Jesus. She did not respond at all, so I do not know whether she understood me; but I do pray that God the Holy Spirit would open her heart to receive the message of love and mercy, though so feebly and imperfectly delivered.

"The two children are dear little things, very quick, and so good in attending to their studies. They always come down to the door with me, each holding a hand, and when we are descending the narrow staircase, they prefer going sideways rather than release their hold of me. When we get to the door they shake hands, and stand making salaams until I drive away.

"Poor little girls! it is only till they are married that they are allowed to come to the door. After that event they are closely shut up. I could almost wish them to remain children."

Again—"I have opened a new house lately, in which there are twelve ladies who learn. It would amuse you if you could see them crowding round me. The house is an immense one, and it requires the organ of locality to find one's way into the women's apartments. I have to pass through court after court, and then I peep into one room after another, catching one lady asleep, one dressing, one reading over her lesson, two or three chatting over the events of the day, &c. As soon as they see me, up they jump; and soon they are all assembled in our 'schoolroom,' and we set to work. The second day I visited this house I had such a nice talk with the ladies.

"There were no chairs in the room I was shown into, so I sat down on a mattress on the floor, and the women immediately crowded round me, holding my hands, and sometimes my feet!

"Then I began to tell them of Jesus, and they listened attentively; if I stopped for a moment, they said, 'Tell us more, tell us more.' A friend who was with me said, 'What a picture you would make for England if I could take you!'"

Again—"This zenana is at the end of a long, narrow lane, so I have to get out of my ghari, and walk some distance. One day I was walking, gazing with longing eyes at the zenanas I passed on the way, when I heard a window opened above me, and an entreating voice in Bengali, 'Mem, Mem,* won't you come and see us?' You can imagine how delighted I was to go, and how I ran up the very narrowest staircase I ever saw in my life, through various little verandahs and rooms, till I found myself eagerly welcomed by seven or eight women, all wanting to catch hold of me at once. They dragged me into a room, took off my hat, and put me into a chair before I could say a word. They then seated themselves round me, and began asking questions as to where I lived. Would not I always come to see them? &c.

"They told me they had heard of me through the servants, who told them of a 'Mem' who went to a house at the end of the lane; so they had watched and called me in as I told you. I was greatly pleased with them all. Some few days afterwards, when in this house, I heard some invisible person call 'Mem, Mem!' and for some time could not discover where the voice came from.

"On opening a window, however, I saw two or three people standing on a housetop, and several other women peeping out of the door opening on the top of the house. They called out, 'Come to us,' and when I went, received me warmly. I found

* The title given in India to a European lady.

some of the ladies could read a little, and all seemed anxious to learn. I cannot, however, *teach* there yet, for the Babu will not give his consent; but I think perhaps I may get it soon.

"While sitting in this house, a servant came from a neighbouring one, begging me to go and see her mistress; so I crept out of the little door before mentioned, scrambled over the roof, followed by my new friends, and we entered the house by a similar doorway (a place not much bigger than the port of a ship's cabin). I was just as warmly received here, and was so pleased to find that this lady would really learn. I go to her regularly now; and the other day when there, I was greatly amused by hearing a tremendous knocking on a wooden window, and voices saying—

"'Is the Mem here? Open, that we may see her!'

"The shutters were soon opened, and then three bright faces gazed at me through the bars; it was so amusing to hear their remarks to one another on my appearance. I have seven houses in that lane. Is not that delightful? Though they do not all learn, yet I go and talk to them; and it is so cheering to see how they look for me, and how anxious they are to keep me with them, sometimes holding my hat that I may not go away."

CHAPTER X.

THE DIVERSITIES OF CLIMATE, LANGUAGE, ETC.

BEFORE continuing our visits to the zenana-homes of our Hindu sisters, it seems desirable to remind our readers of the vastness of the land over which our thoughts travel when we speak of India.

Nearly two thousand miles in length from north to south, and upwards of fifteen hundred in breadth from east to west, it includes among its many peoples and tribes variations and differences which it is difficult to realise when speaking of one country. With more than twenty different languages and dialects, and therefore with no common bond of intercourse; with several distinct religious systems, Hindu, Parsi, Mohammedan, and others; with variations of climate, from the Himalayan snows to the intensest tropical heat, it is impossible to give descriptions of *any* institution, phase of society, customs, habits, dress, &c., which would apply to *every part* of the country *alike*.

Allowance must be made for infinite varieties, shades of difference, and peculiarities, as influenced by locality, necessities of climate, different religious ideas, and intercourse with the outside world. Thus it will be understood that we can only give broad and general ideas, leaving it to our readers to fix the varieties in their proper places, as they study the different stations alluded to. Thus "the zenana" is not a term *used* all over India. In fact, it is scarcely heard in the south, though the seclusion it implies is understood, and, alas! practised all over this vast empire.

There are many different terms to express the same idea. In Delhi and the north they speak of "purdah"—*i.e.*, curtained women—or of keeping purdah, whilst in the central provinces they call it keeping "gosha;" but in Bengal, and wherever the Bengalis are located, the term zenana has been adopted, though the real Bengali word is "anthakar."

Everywhere it *means* the same thing, namely, that women are not to be trusted, but must be shut up as birds in a cage—must be hidden from the sight of all but their own husbands. The why? the wherefore? and the effect of such treatment being, alas! obvious enough, and terribly deplorable. Yet it is only lately that we have begun to realise, *even in the faintest degree*, the thickness of the gloom in which these poor women have been for so many long centuries immersed.

Now as we visit from house to house, perhaps we can gather fresh ideas of both themselves and their homes, which will quicken us into warmer sympathy and more earnest prayer.

The difficulty of making word pictures vivid and realisable is of course great, still we must try. Here is a description from a missionary friend, who had felt the same difficulty:—"I had often wondered why one had such a dim impression of what a zenana was like, and wished for a minute description. I now wonder no longer. A zenana is simply indescribable, from the fact that no two are alike, and not one seems to have been built on any supposable plan or shape.

"A collection of dirty courtyards, dark corners, break-neck staircases, filthy outhouses and entries, overlaid with rubbish, or occupied by half-clad native servants, stretched about on charpoys, or on the ground indifferently—narrow verandahs, and unfurnished, or semi-furnished, and very small rooms. Such is a zenana and its surroundings. The approach to the house is often so intricate, rough, or small, that it becomes an impossibility for the ghari* to approach, and one must go on foot—a perilous proceeding under the scorching rays of a tropical sun.

"Once inside the zenana, you are struck, as a rule, by the entire absence of all that constitutes to our ideas the complement of a room—its furniture. Tables and chairs are not to be thought of, *except when brought in from the Babu's† apartments*, for the teacher's use *for the time being*. In one room a sheet was spread on the floor, and little bolsters all around, for the afternoon nap!

"Generally speaking, the lessons are given and received in the open verandah; and while one or two are learning, the remainder of the feminine occupants

* Wheeled conveyance. † The gentleman's.

of the house squat themselves down on the ground to stare and make their remarks on the foreigner. You can at once discern, by the marvellous improvement in the manners, which of the ladies have been under instruction for any length of time."

This was written of the Calcutta zenanas. A missionary from Banares writes—"The homes here are more gloomy, dirty, and devoid of every comfort than in Calcutta. Even at this cold season the majority of the women wear no other clothing than their thin saris, and sit on the cold mud or flag floors with their uncovered legs or feet, so that one wonders they are not constantly suffering from rheumatism."

And another writes—"The women have always the worst part of the house assigned them, and seem to have few comforts given them. Even in the large residences of the rich Babus, one can always tell when getting near the rooms allotted to the women, by the dirty miserable appearance of the walls, staircases, and courts.

"Many of the high-caste natives are very poor, and then they have to live in small wretched houses; but some of them are rich, their dwellings are large and airy, and furnished with luxuries; but the ladies do not share in the comforts, though they may be better dressed, and have more servants to wait on them. This does not speak much for the chivalry of the men; and, alas! the outside dirt and carelessness is but a type of the actual neglect and oppression."

A HINDU WOMAN'S COMPLAINT.

One of our pupils said the other day, " Oh, if you only knew the lives of us Hindu women, and all we have to suffer, you could not help weeping for us ! "

And again, a lady visitor writes—" It is quite sad to see those young creatures tied down for life, by marrying before they ought to be out of the nursery; and they get to look so old! I was astonished to learn that many whom I took for twenty-five or more, are only fourteen or fifteen years of age.

" In one of my zenanas the lessons are somewhat interrupted on account of the baby being constantly ill. I quite grieve to hear the poor little thing fret all the time I am in the house; and the worst of it is, that I believe if a good dhai, or wet nurse, could be obtained, the child would be better—but alas for caste! One of the right sort cannot be found, so the poor baby's life is risked. I talked seriously to the mother about it yesterday, but she said she must think of what her relations would say. The old lady rather denied the matter of caste, and said no dhai of any caste could be got; but I fear the daughter's was the real version—dread of the scorn of others. *The baby is a little girl*, and so not cared for as if it had been a boy, as is always the case in this country. A boy is a mother's pride, and a girl is often only an endurance; partly, I believe, the reason is, that the girl goes out of the family when she marries, while the son remains and brings home his wife. It is very likely, however, that the women in many instances feel the misery of their own lives, and know that their daughters have but the same prospect."

Again—"The little child-wife, a child but eight years of age, was disobedient to the mother-in-law: she went to her own home, and then refused to return to her husband's home. This stopped my visits for a fortnight; for, having sent several times, the mother-in-law said she would send no more; when the Babu came home the little wife must be punished. Whether she was coaxed or frightened into a return, I do not know, as I did not like to ask on my next visit, she being present; though, after our lesson, I told her she must not run away for so long any more, and tried to get her to understand the duty of obedience. Poor little wife!"

A friend, writing of the wife of one of our missionaries whom she had just seen, says, "She seems so bright and earnest. I am sure the zenana ladies will like her; they thoroughly appreciate cheerfulness, *so depressed and oppressed are they*." And another writes—"I have one new Bengali house. I had some difficulty in persuading the Babu, a *very* wise, intelligent man, of very high caste, to let me go to this house. He said it was such a wretched one, his own being under repair; but he yielded at last, and on Monday asked me to see him about some other houses. And then he said that his family were delighted at my visits, and *not the least afraid*, but looked on me quite as a friend. I have eight in this house—*quite a small school*, and so bright and merry; they joke with each other, and laugh and talk, so that I come away quite exhausted with the teaching and the talking, and the effort to keep them anything like serious; yet I cannot help feeling pleased to see this *new* phase of native life, *one so rarely sees a merry woman*."

CHAPTER XI.

THE IGNORANCE AND PREJUDICE OF THE WOMEN.

IT is not surprising that ignorance and prejudice hinder and beset our efforts on every side; the real wonder would be if it were otherwise. The poor women themselves have to struggle through every sort of traditional barrier, which would still bind them in chains of ignorance and superstition. Here are some specimens of this phase of the work—"After my first visit to one zenana, the old mother broke every water-vessel in the house, believing I had made them impure; and I understand she has drunk no water since, *except what she has herself fetched from the Ganges*—the Holy River. The natives are all *most particular* about water; if I give medicine, they will take it, *but not if I put it into water*, or into any but their own vessel."

Again—"Some of the women are dreadfully slow, and learn at such a snail's pace that one is almost tempted to despair. But then, what can be expected of those whose minds have been a barren waste up to the age of thirty or forty? Some, when we begin to teach them, cannot even count above thirty or forty; and one woman, when I showed her the maps, and explained the construction and material of the earth, moon, and stars, gravely asked if the world I came from was made of land or water! Another feared to come near me, asking our native teachers if I were a man or a woman? These being our *materials*, it would be strange indeed if the heights of knowledge were reached by flying leaps, but not the results we wait in faith for, God's promises being the assurances of our success."

And again—"One of my favourite houses is closed, the lady being in great anxiety about her little baby. She has already lost four little ones, and I fancy she is afraid lest a Christian's presence may bring about the loss of this one. In another house *this is the openly avowed reason* for the lady not learning now, that since she began to learn she has lost her children, and so her husband has forbidden my visits. My heart often aches for these dear women, who have to suffer in sickness, and bereavements and trials of many kinds, and who have no comfort, no hope, no resting-place, no covert from the storm."

Another missionary writes—"Lately a few of our houses have closed, the friends taking alarm at the interest in Christianity shown by those under instruction. One is the house of a bigoted Mohammedan. His daughter was a very idle girl, a great opium-eater; consequently listless and inert. Half the time one was there, she would either be sleeping or painting her eyelids, doing her hair, &c., so that I had small hope of her making much progress; but her cousin, our other pupil, was a bright, intelligent girl, and I was very sorry to lose her. However, they have each a Bible in their own tongue, and some day God may be pleased to bless its message to some soul within that dark house."

Let us now speak of

PROGRESS.

For, however dark and sad these pictures may be, the very fact that we *can* speak of them, that we have made our way inside these prison-houses, is a token of success, and the earnest of better days to these "prisoners of hope." Let it be remembered, that, wherever our missionaries go, there they carry "the Word," "the entrance of which giveth light," and we shall be able to wait with patient hope for a fuller awakening.

Meanwhile, such descriptions as the following are cheering:—"In one house there is a family of five ladies—two little girls, and three grown-up women, —and it is most interesting to see this family assembled for their lessons, and the eagerness of them all. They are always prepared, with their books and work laid nicely on the table. It is not usual for them to have tables and chairs; but now, in almost all the zepanas in which we teach, they have civilised their places, and make everything nice and ready for us, and they seem to take a real interest in their learning. They learn verses out of the Bible, and those who can read at all have Bibles of their own, and some of them read it with great delight.

"It seems to me that they are beginning to get hold

of things by the *right end* now, and to be finding out that the real difference between us lies not in our *skin*, but in our *religion.* They begin to feel there is something higher in religion than merely trying to propitiate the powers of evil. They begin to *think*, to *wonder*, and to *ask questions;* but there are great difficulties in the way still. There are the *old ladies* in every family—the grandmothers, and great-grandmothers, the white-haired, venerable-looking personages (old ladies), *who sit and look*, if they are not blind, *and listen*, if they are not deaf; and even if they are both blind and deaf, they know that there is something new going on in their families, and some spirit moving about which never moved *them* in their youth.

Their daughters-in-law no longer sit all day long, as was their wont, counting their jewels or combing their hair; there is a rousing up of mind and body which they cannot understand, and the mothers raise a warning finger to tell them to beware! the gods will be displeased; their children will die—their religion, the ancient religion of their forefathers, will be destroyed—they are going to be made Christians. For many years longer such warnings will be heard from the ancient ladies of every family, and will, no doubt, be listened to with the superstitious respect almost always accorded to these white-headed spirits of the zenanas. But still much progress is made; and even the oldest bigots must be softened in time by the happy, interested faces and busy hands where ignorance and idleness were wont to reign."

Again—"The contrast between those zenanas where female education is progressing, and those who will not have it, is very remarkable. In the one you see the ladies sitting in the sun, with their knees drawn up to the chin, *absolutely* idle. In the other you go in and find the whole female part of the family with their books and work around; some learning their lessons, mothers and daughters *together;* some working; others, it may be, reading; those who are able to read well and easily, reading a story-book, such as 'Faith and Victory,' 'The Dairyman's Daughter,' and other little books which have been translated into their language; but you seldom find them idle, and they are so much more cheerful and happy, as a rule, than they were in their days of indolence. Some little rays of Christian light have certainly broken in on them, and for this may we not be thankful?"

We will now give a Hindu puja or worship scene, and then pass on to a few extracts regarding the work amongst the Mohammedans.

A PUJA SCENE.

"A few mornings ago, in one of the zenanas, the mother of our pupils came into the court with a lota full of water in one hand, and a flower-saucer, containing loose petals of a beautifully-scented white flower which grows here very abundantly in the other. She made her way to one corner of the court, where stood a flower in a large pot; this she sprinkled over with the white petals, then watered it from the 'lota. Folding her hands together, she walked several times round the pot, muttering some prayers which I could not make out; she then prostrated herself, letting her forehead touch the ground two or three times. She afterwards came forward to offer her salaams with a look of most thorough satisfaction. *At that very moment* the three younger members of the family were being taught 'God so loved the world, that He gave His only-begotten Son, that whosoever believeth in Him should not perish, but have everlasting life.'"

THE MOHAMMEDANS AND THEIR PECULIARITIES.

Let us now pay some visits to the Mohammedan ladies—Begums (literally, princesses) as they are styled—and of whom our friend writes—"They are even more like prisoners than the Hindus, if that be possible." And another—"I do feel greatly interested in the Mohammedans, and very thankful to see the least sign of a desire for knowledge among them. They are such a listless, indifferent kind of people, that it is always hard to calculate on them as pupils; even in one of the most promising houses a young Begum said to me this morning, 'If I do learn to read, and learn everything else that you wish me, what use will it be? What shall I get for it? My brother can earn something by it, but of what use will it be to me?'"

The wife of a German missionary in Lucknow tells us of some of her visits thus:—"A respectable but poor family have asked me to visit them; and when I did so, they took me up to the little roof. The wife of a neighbour saw me there, and begged me to come to her also, so I proposed to the other ladies to go. Now the ladies of Lucknow have little holes through which they pay each other, in private, friendly visits. I had never crept through so small an aperture, and got such a knock on my head as almost stunned me and pained me for weeks afterwards." The same friend writes—"I have never seen any zenana that had the slightest pretence to be called a *home.* Each lady adorns herself (except those who, through despair or opium, have got into a state of apathy); they look after their finery and jewels, and their pretty paint-boxes; but the house is nobody's, and nobody cares for *it.*

"The entrance to one of the zenanas I visited was through a narrow gutter. When I had traversed this abominable passage, I came into a very small paved courtyard, horribly dirty! Carefully, from stone to stone, I picked my way to a narrow staircase in the wall, coming upon the small but clean terrace; and there, like a bed of gorgeous tulips, sat the Begums dressed in the gayest silks and muslins, sparkling with jewels, and giving me a most cordial welcome.

"In one of my visits a young Begum told me she had been longing to see me, and wished to ask me some questions. The chief of these was, 'How was marriage conducted, and the rite looked upon, by Christians?' I gave them a full explanation of the holy duties of married life, and how our Saviour had restored the institution to what it had been intended by our heavenly Father it should be. They all listened very attentively and silently; though sometimes they could not restrain their admiration at the Christian regulations and doctrines.

Then said the young Begum, 'Now I will tell you how it is with us. Have you ever seen a man take a goat, tie it with a string, and give it to another man? Just so are we given away; no one knows, is my husband good or bad, shall I be happy or miserable. And our men are very bad; you can have no notion of it; among a thousand there is not one good man.' I pointed out to them how the Lord alone could comfort them, how they should pour out their sorrows to Him; and then with a very sad heart I took my leave of them."

CHAPTER XII.

MORE EXTENDED OBSERVATIONS.

HITHERTO our details and sketches have been chiefly drawn from our accounts of work in North India. Now we will travel southwards, noting points of interest as we go on, thanking God that the spirit of awakening is moving all over the country, from north to south, from east to west. We can hope too that through His goodness it will never be laid to sleep again, but that rather it will shake mightily each corner of the land until the present darkness and ignorance shall be things of the past—until knowledge and truth shall reign, and India be won for our waiting Lord.

A Bombay correspondent writes—"Very few, if any, of the upper class Hindu or Mussulman ladies are allowed to go outside their own houses. I have been often through the bazaars, and have seen *but one;* of the lower classes there are plenty, of course, as they have to go about their daily business.

The Parsi ladies, however, do come out; I have seen several. One evening I heard a band playing in the compound, belonging to a wealthy Parsi, and found the ladies were dancing away, just as English ladies might have done on any special holiday. Nevertheless, if the accounts of their houses are correct, they are very far from being properly civilised.

It was a curious sight the day our new Viceroy landed, the varieties amongst the crowds of spectators being very striking: the European ladies—the various uniforms amongst the Englishmen; and then the differences amongst the native gentlemen, Hindus, Parsis, Mohammedans, Thibetians, Punjabis, natives from every part of India, in all sorts of costumes; but with the exception of a few Parsi women in carriages, *I did not see a single native lady*."

THE TRAVELS OF SOME HINDU LADIES.

A friend interested in missionary labour, journeying to Europe by steamer, thus describes a scene she witnessed:—" On arriving off Madras, signals from the shore induced the captain to pause, and a boat was seen to put off and make its way to the ship. On nearing, it was found to contain a native gentleman and a number of native servants, also a palanquin; and one end of tho boat was closely covered in.

" The captain had previously been informed that a native gentleman wished to travel with his wives to Mecca, and that he would bring them thus to the vessel. Cabins had of course been secured; and now, the boats being alongside, the gentleman stepped on deck with two or three of the native servants; the cabins were inspected, and then the palanquin was raised to the deck, and, still closely shut up, was carried to the cabin, and its occupant deposited there.

"Again and again it was lowered to the boat, bringing up each time from out of its covered end another of the wives, and afterwards their female attendants. Each solitary occupant was immediately carried to the cabin below, and there closely secured. At last all were on board, and the vessel once more on its way; the native gentleman and his male servants mingling freely with the other passengers, the poor ladies being left alone below.

"This continued for several days, in spite of the entreaties of the English lady passengers to be allowed to relieve the monotony of their poor encaged sisters, until one evening, when, at the suggestion of the captain, all the gentlemen passengers were requested to remain on deck, and a brief hour of liberty was granted to the imprisoned women, who were allowed to come out into the saloon, and wonder and laugh at the strange things they saw, and chat with such of the English ladies as understood enough of the native languages to make themselves understood.

"The short hour was soon gone, and then they hurried again to their hiding-place, to leave the saloon and the rest of the vessel to its former occupants.

This scene was repeated from time to time in the course of the voyage, until, arriving at the city of Mecca, whither they were bound, the palanquin was again brought into requisition, and the "travelled" Hindu ladies were closely shut up in it, and carried to a fresh zenana, where they were expected and prepared for by other imprisoned friends."

Does such a voyage suggest nothing deeper than its picture of a group of "purdah women?" Can English hearts stand calm and silent whilst womanhood is thus degraded? But it is not the outside troubles and trials only we so greatly deplore; it is the ignorance, superstition, and moral degradation which is so terrible to contemplate and so difficult to overcome. Let us now give a few instances of prevailing ignorance and superstition.

IGNORANCE AND SUPERSTITION.

A zenana teacher writes—"In one of my visits I took with me a doll which I had brought out from England. Having arrived at a prison-like house, we went up a steep, dark, narrow staircase, and reached the roof, where we found the assembled family of women. There were seven or eight of different ages—from an old grandmother of sixty to a young girl of thirteen.

"They received us gladly. The doll excited great admiration; they gazed in wonder at her china face and blue eyes, and were delighted to see her dressed and undressed. They asked her price, and the old woman wanted to know if she had ever been a little child! They nursed and petted her, and put on her hat, and would have been well pleased to keep her. Poor creatures! it is sad to see them so childish and frivolous. They listened to a few serious words, and I am well assured would gladly listen to more, but for their lords and masters, who well know that when once their women are educated they will be beyond their power."

Another says—"Sometimes I take my morning walk towards the wells, in a shady dell, and there converse with the women who come to draw water. This morning a group of three or four were standing with their ghurras, or earthen vessels, lying on the ground. One of the women thought I touched a neighbour's vessel with my foot, and exclaimed, 'See, she has polluted it; you must break your ghurra;' but the other women protested that, though near, I had not touched it. They did not appeal to me, for which I was glad, and so the pot was saved."

Again—"In a visit to a new house, I was introduced to a widowed mother and her two daughters-in-law. The mother seemed pleased to receive us, and was interested in looking at a few specimens of fancy-work, but did not care to learn, saying, 'The tailor makes our clothes; why should I work?' I then read one of Barth's Bible stories, and after talking about it, asked if she did not think it would be pleasant to be able to read for herself, or to teach her little boys who were playing around her. She answered, 'What should I learn to read for? If I can cook a good dinner, that is all I am required to do, and the boys go to school.'"

A Bombay friend writes—"When speaking to one of my pupils on the desirability of learning to read, she exclaimed, 'How do you expect we can ever learn to do anything you do? You sit on chairs, we on the floor; you have knives and forks, we eat with our fingers; you have cooks, we have to prepare our own food. No, no; we can never learn to do anything you do.' At length I was able to lead her to see that reading and thinking did not necessarily imply chairs or knives and forks, and that books might be more within her compass than she imagined."

Then again—"On going to one house I found they had been out, so I asked them where they had been. To Kardha, to worship a goddess, said one, and were there all night, adding that this goddess would give anything if a vow was made to her. I told them that she was only a stone, and had no virtue in her, and that there is only one true God, who has created us all. 'No, no,' they replied; '*she* is the only true god, the true god above all.' I talked to them much about the foolishness of idolatry, but they were staunch in their belief of this goddess.

"I have one small house where I have no need to

take a picture or anything else to pave the way to the subject of religion. Small as it is, I have a great many learners there; but there is one old woman not a pupil, who nevertheless, whenever she sees me coming, immediately joins the party, and begins by saying she has come for a talk. Last time I went she began at once on the respective merits of their deities as compared with our Saviour's. She chose Durga as the theme of her eulogies. Now you would think there could be no difficulty in at once showing the superiority of our all-powerful and yet gentle loving Saviour, 'who went about doing good,' to the bloodthirsty, cruel Durga; but you must remember these poor women have been brought up to look upon Durga as all-powerful, and it would be difficult to prove to them the invalidity of the great works said to have been done by her, and the validity of the mighty and merciful works of our Saviour. At last, when she had had her answers to every argument I put forth, deeply feeling my weakness, I asked for wisdom to answer her; and the answer was, I am sure, given me.

"I said to her, 'Well, you believe in the power of your cruel Durga, while I am fully convinced of the might of our loving Jesus, and do not believe in Durga's having any power whatever; however, I will believe in it if you can give me this proof of her power. Show me *one* of your countrymen who will, simply for the *love* of Durga, forsake his family, friends, and country, and with expense and trouble to himself, cross the seas to go and convince my country-people of the power of Durga or his love for her.

"The poor woman was completely silenced; and when all the listeners looked to her for a reply, she said, 'Ah, that is a hard question;' and then, though she had showed no signs of being in any hurry before, she hastily added, 'I have no more time for talk to-day; I have work to do at home.' Poor woman! I feel specially interested in her, because I scarcely ever see her without her saying, 'Ah well, if your Jesus will give me the faith, I will believe in Him.' This is true, and I have prayed and longed that it might please Him to do so. She is evidently quite looked up to by the other women."

"Last week," says a lady, "we spent a day at the 'Happy Valley,' and the shade was so thick, we were able to sit out of doors by the side of the brook in the middle of the day without suffering from the sun. But even in this retired spot there were traces of the idolatry which covers the land. On several of the rocks and stones were daubs of red paint, showing that some poor creatures had there offered that homage to stones which belongs to God alone. Red paint converts any object into a god. At the head of the valley stands a rather noted Hindu temple, and its one small room contains a hideous image."

Sugguna writes thus:—"At present there is a great Hindu festival going on of 'Gunputti' (the elephant-headed god); all these things are great hindrances to our work. At such times the women are all excited, and busy preparing sweet bread, &c. Will you come with me, and visit some of the Hindu families, and see what is going on? The houses are of the higher classes, and we know the one we are going to. The child perhaps sees us coming, and runs in to give notice; then those who are asleep rise, for we go at their leisure-time, noon. Others come out from their rooms, and sometimes a neighbour or a friend drops in.

"Our usual seat is a wooden swing, with all the women sitting on the floor beside us. In this particular house the *mother*, *daughter*, and *cousin* are all widows, and look so miserable with their heads shaven, and neither jackets, bangles, or ornaments. While another daughter is as good as a widow; for her husband, who is a doctor, has become a Christian, and she does not wish to follow him. One of these widows, but for the power of English government, would have gladly followed her husband to the funeral pile, and have been burnt with him.

"But to return. After the first words of inquiry are over, we see the 'Gunputti' in state. The best corner in the front room is especially prepared for the god's reception, with paintings and drawings on the wall; this has been the womens' work. A painted mud image, half elephant, half man, is placed on a high pedestal, with all sorts of surroundings within railings; busts, statues of human beings, and everything that they think beautiful or ornamental, has been either bought or borrowed to do it honour. It has also a large plate of sweetmeats, fruit, and flowers placed before it, just as if it could eat. Lights and incense are burning; the Brahman priest attends to read the sacred book and perform the puja; and all the neighbours come in to admire and do homage to the idol.

"After its stated days are over—one and a half, five, ten, or at the most twenty-one—the image is carried away in a palanquin in great pomp, with a band of musicians, and children handsomely dressed, either on richly-caparisoned horses or in grand carriages. The whole procession moves slowly forward to the sea-side, and then poor 'Gunputti' is thrown in. At such times we cannot expect a quiet hearing from the women, nor have they time to read to us, except when they have no 'Gunputti.'"

Another writes—"I asked them what god they worshipped, and they replied, 'Mahadeva.'

"'What is he made of?'

"'Of iron,' they answered.

"'Do you worship him every day?'

"'No; only on our festival-days; on other days he is kept in a small basket, tied with cotton ropes, and hung up to the roof of the house.'

"'How is this?' I added. 'You tie up your god, and he does not say anything or complain? Believe me, Mahadeva is not a true god, he is only made by your hands. The one true God is everywhere; He it is who made heaven and earth, and all things in them; and it is a great sin for us to give God's glory and the reverence due only to Him to this piece of iron.' They paid great attention, and confessed they did not know this true God."

CHAPTER XIII.

MEDICAL MISSIONS.

CHRISTIAN education has already done much for some of the women of India in various parts of the great Continent, and many a zenana has been opened by means of this key. It has, however, failed to find much entrance into Mohammedan homes, for with laudable exceptions, they do not, as a class, appreciate education like the Hindus, and they are, as a mass, ill-affected towards the British Government, which has supplanted their own. But a plan has been thought of, and is now being carried out, equally adapted to both classes, and therefore valuable politically as well as religiously; and oh! how needed for the relief of bodily sufferings.

We notice repeated allusions to sickness in the journals of the zenana teachers, whose pupils are ready to receive with open arms any daughter of the West who comes to assuage her pains and bind up her wounds. Countless mothers and children fall victims to the conceit and ignorance of their female attendants, and of their Hakims, or native doctors. The death-roll among them is enormous; and when a beloved wife or darling child is sick unto death, a medical lady is welcomed as an angel of mercy, and is often successful in bringing relief. Not long ago a missionary was on a preaching-tour among the villages of a remote district in North-West India. He fell ill with fever, and was nursed by his wife, in a small hut on the summit of a lofty hill. The medicines she had with her were blessed to him, and the fever abated.

The tidings spread to the village, and one afternoon a party of Mohammedan women, headed by the wife of the Khan, or chief, climbed the steep ascent, and stood before the "Mem." On her going to meet them, this lady-chief—tall, dignified, and richly jewelled—stepped forward, holding out a rupee, which the "Mem" touched in token of friendship. After many compliments, she said, "Will not the 'Mem,' who has given medicine to her own husband, give some to mine, who has been delirious many days from fever? If she would, he would get well, as her own Sahib is now doing?" She was told of Him who alone has the power to heal, and the lady asked to be allowed to see the sick man; but that could not be permitted, for the villagers feared witchcraft. She then gave the medicine, and the party left.

The next morning the wife of the Khan again appeared with a large retinue of women, all veiled. She was come to express her thanks, for her husband was relieved; and now she was all anxiety for the "Mem" to go and see him, and many other sick ones besides.

The fear of witchcraft was overcome; most joyfully did the "Mem" comply, and descended the rock, followed by her crowd of visitors. She found the Khan on his charpoy, under a shed in the open air, and around him such a muster of sick and suffering ones as she hardly supposed a village could produce, some ill themselves, others bringing their sick friends. There was a general demand for medicine, which was dealt out to each, and taken on the spot; and when all were served, they were told of the Physician of souls, who could heal both bodily and spiritual disease. Most attentively did they listen, and when the "Mem" ceased, they loaded her with gifts of eggs, vegetables, &c., *as presents*, which they had refused to *sell* to her on her arrival, when she needed such supplies very sorely. When she and her husband finally departed, a large company of the villagers went some distance with them, and parted from them with repeated salaams and benedictions.

We have given this anecdote as an illustration of the power of medicine in overcoming Mohammedan prejudice; and it shows that while education is one key, a medical mission is another, to unlock closed entrances both in city and village life. Female medical missions are indeed a key to fit every lock; and she who practises the healing art may hope not only to cure, but to Christianise her patients. She will soften bigotry, remove prejudice, dispel ignorance, drive away gloom, and deposit the leaven of the Gospel in numberless hearts and homes.

Convinced of the importance of this branch of the work, it has been decided by several of the associations sending out female missionaries, to make it a part of their special object. The Americans have set the example in their own energetic way, and "THE INDIAN NORMAL SCHOOL AND INSTRUCTION SOCIETY" are following in their wake. The American ladies are completely educated, and have taken a medical degree. Their plan is not only to practise themselves, but to form a medical school in some central points, and there to educate native women, many of whom are gifted for such work. "THE INDIAN NORMAL SCHOOL AND INSTRUCTION SOCIETY" are, for the present, just sending ladies who have gained sufficient knowledge to be very useful. The two first were designated to Bombay and Banares. The lady for the latter place died suddenly on her voyage out, and the former a few months after her arrival, so that for the present no real work can be alluded to in this branch in connection with the Society.*

An incident from the notebook of a medical missionary will illustrate the value of such work:—

"This morning a Brahman suddenly appeared at my door, one of the most popular and affable men of his caste. His lips were quivering with emotion. 'You are a mother,' he exclaimed; 'I have brought my wife, the mother of my six children, for you to save her. She has been gored by a cow, and only you can help us.'

* The Society for Promoting Female Education, &c., are also taking up this branch of work.

"I went out, and there in a bullock-cart sat the sufferer, her sons beside her, from the youth of sixteen to the babe of two years; the old grandmother and the jewelled daughters trudging tremblingly behind. We led the poor woman gently in; it was a ghastly wound, and she was faint. The silence was broken by the husband asking in agony if I could save her? 'If God blesses my efforts, and you promise to use no heathen incantations should fever come on, I may do much for her,' said I, and I dressed the wound. She revived, and they returned home.

"In the evening I went to see her, and found her as I had desired she might be, placed on a cot in their most airy room, and doing well. After attending to her, I spoke on leaving to the group around me thus:—'Here is a woman like me. God has given her children, and given me children. She has had many earthly comforts, and so have I. When I am in trouble, I like to ask Him to help me, and He has, many times. Who can heal this woman so quickly as the great God who made her. I can ask Him to cure her in my own house; but, if you are quite willing, I should like to ask Him here to help us all, that we make no mistakes, and that He will soon restore her.'

"There were four old women listening, and I expected them to demur to this proposal. Wise in their own eyes, they are most tenacious of heathen customs.

"The husband was too polite to refuse, and said,

'Certainly;' adding to the others, 'She is going to praise the Lord.' 'Let her, let her!' cried the old women. I fully expected they would go about some household work at once; but the silence was unbroken. It was a rare privilege to invite the Great and Holy One into that home where He had never been asked. As I finished the prayer, and looked at the sufferer, she was steadfastly gazing at me with one of the pleasantest smiles I ever saw.

"'*I* shall trust no one but you,' she said, with emphasis.

"Every evening the cart has been sent for me; and last night, when I said that there was no necessity for my coming again, that nothing could have been more satisfactory than the rapid healing of the wound, the thanks of all were quite oppressive. I told them of Jesus' miracles, and His readiness to bless every heart loving and trusting Him. The younger ones listened with interest, the wise old women gave civil attention, and the husband looked to me politely and pleasantly, as if I were a harmless enthusiast."

CHAPTER XIV.

SKETCH OF THE AGENCIES IN OPERATION FOR THE BENEFIT OF HINDU FEMALES.

THE SOCIETY FOR PROMOTING FEMALE EDUCATION IN THE EAST.—This most valuable and much-blessed society enjoys the distinguished honour of being the first, in order of time, of all the purely female organisations which have taken root in Great Britain for carrying the Gospel to the women of heathen lands.

It was founded in 1834, and one among its very first correspondents was Mrs Wilson of Calcutta. It has laboured throughout India, as well as in other lands, and some of its best agents have given their strength, some even their lives, for the evangelisation of their Hindu sisters. It was the first to attempt, in 1842, zenana-work (though not then known by that name), by sending a lady to Bombay for the Parsis: thus it has been the pioneer of all subsequent and kindred efforts. It has established a TRAINING-SCHOOL AND HOME FOR ZENANA WORKERS in one of its stations in North-West India,* and has selected agents to be sent out by other missionary societies. The history of its labours in India alone, would fill a large volume with

* Ludiana.

details of the deepest interest, and did space permit, we might give results of its special efforts that would thrill the hearts of our readers; a few of these will appear incidentally interwoven in the history.

Scotland was among the first to follow the example of London in forming a LADIES' ASSOCIATION FOR HEATHEN WOMEN; and in 1843, when the Free Church was separated from the Established in that country, a second and similar association arose there. Great has been the work which the agents sent out by these two societies have accomplished, especially in Calcutta, Madras, Bombay, and Central India, where Scottish missionaries spend their great power and strength in the education of boys. It is this Christian and thorough education which, after years of persevering labour, has so told on the male population, and made them willing and even anxious to gain the same for their wives and daughters.

Pre-eminent among their female missionaries is Mrs Anderson, still labouring at Madras, who went forth in 1845 as Miss Locher, under the auspices of Scottish ladies, although by birth a German-Swiss. Her labours in Madras have told in a wonderful manner on the female population, and to them may be traced much of the success of female education in that Presidency. A farewell address presented to her by native gentlemen some years ago, when she was about to revisit Europe for her health, makes this fact strikingly apparent.

Another of the reflex influences of THE SOCIETY FOR PROMOTING FEMALE EDUCATION IN THE EAST was the formation in 1859 of a similar association attached to the Wesleyans. An influential lady of their body was conversing with a member of the committee of the above society, who urged on her attention the claims of Hindu women. Some years after, this lady was delighted to receive a letter from her Wesleyan friend, informing her that her words had not been lost, and that she could now announce to her the formation of a "LADIES' COMMITTEE FOR AMELIORATING THE CONDITION OF HEATHEN WOMEN" in direct connection with the great "Wesleyan Missionary Society." Moreover, it was from a suggestion by a Wesleyan missionary's wife, who had been sent out in 1840 by the FEMALE EDUCATION SOCIETY, that this new committee was called into action; so that in a double sense the older was the parent of the younger society. The Rev. George Scott, many years a Wesleyan missionary in Sweden, was also useful in aiding to stir up the zeal of Wesleyan ladies at this time, as he had done in Sweden, in the formation of a small association which exists there.

The efforts of the Wesleyans have been chiefly made in South India and Ceylon; but during 1873 one of their missionary widows had her heart drawn out for the secluded ladies of North India, and went to Lucknow, where she is diligently and successfully labouring among them, and many of her pupils receive the tidings of salvation with joy.

One lady in South India is regarded by the educated natives as the parent of all that has been done for their women; and on her having to leave through failure of health, a touching address was presented to her by these gentlemen, expressive of their grateful affection and appreciation of her invaluable services. In the north of Ceylon, where the Tamil language prevails, the success of the Wesleyans has been very marked.

One striking incident in connection with Jaffnapatam we will mention. It relates to the visit of a Tamil woman, Guana Deepa Ammal, a native of Tanjore (memorable as the scene of Schwartz's labours in the last century), who is a most successful *preacher*. She travels, accompanied by her husband and children, and commences her service by singing a Tamil Christian lyric, which is taken up by different members of her family. This occupies twenty minutes, and is followed by Guana laying down certain fundamental Scripture truths, illustrating them by references to well-known Tamil poets, her quotations from whom are chanted, which relieves the attention of her audience. After her propositions are laid down, she draws out her arguments, and winds up by a most touching appeal.

The service is closed by a benediction chanted by all the party in chorus and semi-chorus. Guana attracts very large congregations, Christian and heathen; and when a favourite god, or still more favourite theory, is attacked and mercilessly torn to shreds, slight murmurs are heard, but as a rule no breach of the peace occurs.

The preaching of a Christian Hindu woman is, to say the least, most novel and startling. The father of this lady was a Tanjore poet, a rarely-gifted man and a Christian, whose life was as "a light shining in a dark place." Some of his verses are as tender, touching, and suggestive as any language can produce, especially those on the person, work, and glory of Christ as the Redeemer; so that it is no wonder their recital moves the emotions of a Tamil audience, whose love of poetry is a national passion.

The power of song is a marvellous power in any land, and may win for Christ multitudes of wanderers.* If rightly directed, glorious results may follow a popular presentation of Christian truth after the mode our sister is adopting, one interesting feature of which is, that her effort is spontaneous and free, and manifests what a Hindu woman may be brought to accomplish. We have thus enlarged here, as little connected with the Wesleyan Association is incorporated in the history.

"The Indian Female Normal School and Instruction Society" sprang out of an effort made by some ladies in London in 1851, who formed themselves into a committee to select agents and obtain funds for the Calcutta Normal School. It took its present name in 1861, and from that time decided to embrace the whole of India in the sphere of its efforts. It sent out its first missionary to South India in 1862. Its work is sufficiently apparent in the history. Its agencies are normal schools, zenana visitation, female

* Since these lines were penned, the visit of the American Evangelists has practically demonstrated their truth.

medical missions, Hindu female schools and Bible-women.

The ASSOCIATION OF LADIES connected with the BAPTIST MISSIONARY SOCIETY was formed in 1867. One of its main objects has been a boarding-school for the daughters of the native Christian families able to pay for the liberal education of their children. This institution has been most carefully and efficiently conducted, and has numbered among its pupils many from distant places, who have while under its roof been truly converted to God. In 1870 there were twenty young ladies under instruction in the school. In zenana visitation at Calcutta, Delhi, Banares, and other localities, the agents of this society have been much encouraged, and have reaped first-fruits that have animated their hope of a harvest gathering by and by. In Delhi they have from sixty to a hundred zenanas under visitation, and similar success elsewhere.

The LADIES' ASSOCIATION connected with the oldest of the English missionary societies, that for the PROPAGATION OF THE GOSPEL, was formed in 1866, and has taken its part in Indian work. Their chief station is Delhi, where they have a medical missionary, in addition to their other agencies; and Mrs Winter, their missionary's wife, is one of the most gifted and successful of zenana workers, both among Hindus and Mohammedans. At Cawnpore, where they have long had an orphanage, which has prepared them native helpers, the zenana-work is encouraging; and at Ghazebad also. Nor must we omit Calcutta, with its out-station of Barripur, where to their missionary, as to others, the houses of native gentlemen are rapidly opening. They also work with encouragement in the Madras and Bombay Presidencies.

Christian ladies, in other countries of Europe, soon awoke to the lamentable condition of our Eastern sisters, and GENEVA formed its society. Then came PRUSSIA, and the BERLIN LADIES' SOCIETY has long taken its place as a co-worker, and directs some of its efforts to India. HOLLAND has also an association watching with Christian care over the native women of its Eastern colonies. BELGIUM has offered a first-fruit of the same Christian sympathy. BASEL has an association; and we may add another link to the golden chain by mentioning SWEDEN as also possessing its little band of sisters in Christ, who unite to make known the savour of His name, and have sent forth their missionary agents, few in number but faithful in work, to help to do battle with the mighty foe. The Swedish ladies were moved to action by an earnest appeal from the Rev. Geo. Scott, and by a Swedish missionary, Dr Fjellsledt.

And last, not least, comes the WOMAN'S UNION MISSIONARY SOCIETY OF AMERICA. It was in February 1861 that a voluntary union association for the Christian women of America was formed at New York. It includes all willing to help to raise their degraded sisters in heathen lands. It is literally a WOMEN'S MISSION TO WOMEN, and the only foreign missionary society in America where all can work exclusive of denominational differences.

It sends out single female missionaries to work in three ways:—I. By teaching in zenanas; II. By training and employing native Christian women as Bible-readers, &c.; and, III. By establishing schools for girls. Thirty-six female missionaries have already gone forth to various fields. The second sent out was to Calcutta, where there had been no American mission before her arrival, and where she established a HOME for the training of missionaries now employed there, and in other parts of India. A wide field of labour has not only opened, but been zealously entered by Miss Brittain and her fellow-workers, who can now count nearly two hundred zenanas under their influence, with upwards of twenty day-schools, and many hundreds of pupils in each department.

This association has also female medical missionaries at work, who are much encouraged in their most needed branch of service, especially in North-West India. Though one of the youngest of the societies, it has outstripped in its zealous and successful efforts some of its elder sisters, and has rejoiced over some of the most interesting conversions with which God has crowned the labours of zenana workers.* It is maintained in America with much

* In 1868 Miss Brittain could look on nearly thirty of her zenana pupils as sisters in Christ. The daily life of some of these dear women reminds one in its purity, patient endurance, meek submission, and the "love that suffereth long and is kind," of the description given in a former chapter, of what Shiva says of his wife, and still more touchingly of the gentleness and lowliness of Christ, and of those women who were His faithful followers when on earth.

enthusiasm, especially by children, whose juvenile efforts are marvellously successful in helping its funds. In 1868, in a time of pressure, these zealous little workers collected in a few months no less than 20,960 dollars, or £4146, as the children's offerings.

We here close our brief epitome of the women of India and Christian Work in the Zenana, and add some sketches of a few of the missionary workers who have lived and died in the service of their Hindu sisters.

BIOGRAPHIES.

HANNAH MARSHMAN.

[Born 1767. Died 1847. Missionary Life, forty-eight years.]

We have very little on record of this interesting woman, but, as the first in order of time who attempted any effort for the women of India, we give her the first place in our missionary biographies.

Hannah Shepherd was born at Bristol, in the west of England, in May 1767, and though but eight years old at the time of her mother's death, was so deeply impressed by that mother's holy teaching and example, that the buddings of grace in her heart could be traced to that early period.

In her twelfth year she lost her other parent; but, happily for the orphan child, her grandfather nurtured those seeds of genuine piety which had been sown by the pious mother, and at the age of fifteen it became evident they had germinated, and were producing the fruits of righteousness in her life.

A sickness of three years' duration ripened her graces and matured her character, and thus prepared her for the vocation on which she eventually entered.

The earlier years of her married life were passed very happily as a pastor's wife in Bristol; but suddenly the call came to her husband and herself, as to Abram of old, to forsake their kindred and their father's house, and to go forth to a land which He would show them. The flesh shrank from the sacrifice, immeasurably greater in those early days than now; but faith triumphed, and like Abram they obeyed, scarcely knowing whither they went. Happily for Mrs Marshman, she possessed great constitutional energy and capacity, a temper ardent and enterprising, with the power of forming strong attachments.

To these characteristic endowments for foreign service was added deep religious feeling amounting to enthusiasm, humility, strong faith, and a zeal which no difficulties, no privations, could quench or overcome. What had she not to endure in those early days of missionary labour!

It was in 1799, at the age of thirty-two, accompanied by her young family, that Mrs Marshman landed in India, where, as the wife of one of the best known and most honoured missionaries of modern times, she almost immediately began her attempt to educate those females who were accessible. At Serampur, where she was located, she founded a boarding-school for such girls (of mixed blood) as she could obtain, hoping thus to prepare women ready to work among the natives when schools for them became possible. About seven years later she began a native girls' school—at first for the daughters of the Christian converts, and as prejudice gave way, heathen girls were added. Encouragements were not wanting, though definite results were rare and scanty.

Still she laboured on, and in due time her heart was made glad by perceiving that sister missionaries gained courage to follow her example in Calcutta, with more promise of progress. But the zeal of others only quickened her own, and her natural vigour enabled her to labour on till nearly the end of her life.

How beautifully did that life close in fulness of grace and hope of glory! "Mark the perfect man, and behold the upright, for the end of that man is peace," was verified during the days that closed her earthly pilgrimage. On hearing of a native Christian's exclamation, that his heart leapt for joy whenever he read of Bunyan's pilgrim crossing the river, she said, "I am in that river now; and if you speak of me to the people when I am gone, speak from a text that has been most precious to me, 'He took *me*, and drew me out of many waters,' and read where Christian passes the river."

A little later *she* passed that flood in safety; the shining ones stood ready on the bank to conduct her to the gates of the celestial city, the night-veil of mortality was dropped, and the ransomed soul was for ever clad in the garments of immortality.

Her earthly life extended over eighty years, and her descendants, among whom the children of General Sir Henry Havelock—memorable as the deliverer of Lucknow at the time of the Indian Mutiny—are best known, have risen up to call her blessed, and to confer on India, the land of their parents' adoption, many a rich gift.

HARRIET WINSLOW.

[Born 1796. Died 1833. Went to India 1819. Fourteen years a missionary.]

We can scarcely pass by, in these notices of eminent female missionaries, the name of Mrs Harriet Winslow, though her labours were not so exclusively for women as those of the others whose memoirs are given, nor was her station the continent of India, but Jaffnapatam, in the north of Ceylon.

She had, however, the honour of breaking up fallow ground, and of being one of the first to name the name of Jesus to Cingalese females.

Truly converted to God at thirteen years of age, Harriet Lathrop, of Connecticut, U.S., entered at once with all the freshness of youthful zeal on the service of her Redeemer, and was found ready at nineteen to accept the offer of a missionary to be his fellow-helper in his work; and on reaching the appointed station, she set at once to work in the true spirit of an evangelist.

She writes—"Our dwelling was in a wretched state, but we made some windows by weaving palmyra leaves, basket fashion, across small cords extended from side to side of the frames we had constructed, feeling that as funds were low, we would settle in without floors, doors, or windows, except such as we could make ourselves; and we were quite as comfortable as we expected to be before leaving America. We immediately began to work, and walked forth in the evening to look for natives. The first two women we saw were respectable, and of high caste.* They were very civil, and engaged to come to our house this afternoon, to hear something very interesting we had to tell them. A man who stood by said, 'No, they must not go; they have many relations, and cannot go without them.'

"The next house that we visited was in a cluster of huts, where quite a company of women assembled on hearing our voices. Several promised to attend our meeting. Ten of them, with two others, came this afternoon, when no men were present. They were very attentive, while we told them what induced us to leave our friends and come to live among them, and tried to convince them that the soul will not inhabit the body of some animal after death, but live for ever with God, or wicked men and angels. One of them asked, 'Shall *we* go to heaven or hell?' You may judge how deeply interested they felt in this question, when I tell you that we had scarcely begun to reply when they became restless and went away. This is more than we commonly have to encourage us. Few will listen attentively

* Ladies are not secluded in Ceylon as in Bengal and North-West India, and females of all classes have more liberty there than on the Continent,—perhaps because Buddhism is the prevailing religion, not Brahmanism.

for the shortest time. They know nothing and fear nothing. Their mental degradation is indescribable, and they are contented with it."

This was a first lesson, the next was more encouraging. In less than two years from this time some hundreds of girls were under Christian instruction in day and boarding schools; women were among the converts, and a maternal society was formed, of which Mrs Winslow was secretary.

This association was blessed in various ways. It is referred to in a letter of subsequent date, where, after giving a minute account of the engagements of her self-denying day, she adds—"In relation to our evenings, I might say that on Sabbath evenings we have a meeting with the children and servants; Monday evening a season of social prayer for ourselves and our dear Charles; Wednesday evening, with all the missionaries, we devote to prayer for a blessing on our work, in connection with the missionaries in Bombay; and Saturday evening, from eight to nine, is a concert of prayer by the members of the maternal society, for our children. We have, until the last two weeks, had a meeting for inquirers one or two evenings in the week, which we now have on Tuesday afternoon, and sometimes again on Friday." She then remarks—"There is still time to do much for the women, which must be done by us exclusively."

Two years later a school for girls, whose education was intended to prepare them for teachers, was added to one that had already been founded for boys, and twenty-nine children of good promise came under

Mrs Winslow's care, in addition to the boarding and day schools before alluded to. Much earnest prayer was offered for these girls, and the Lord worked powerfully on the hearts of many, so that not only pupils but teachers and servants shared the blessing, and a goodly number came out as disciples of the Lord Jesus, rejoicing the heart of His faithful servant. Nearly fifty individuals were the permanent fruits of this blessed movement, a good proportion of whom were girls from this school.

In the year following, 1825, Mrs Winslow's health entirely gave way, the inevitable effect of labours like hers in a tropical climate. A change to another part of India was blessed to its restoration; but other and very cutting trials followed—among them sore bereavements of attached fellow-workers, and of several of her own beloved children. Under the mellowing influence of grief, as well as the strengthening effects of joy, the fruits of the Spirit ripened as rain and sunshine succeeded each other in her experience; but bodily vigour again suffered, and new power for active effort much diminished.

In 1830 her heart was again made glad by the outbreak of a work of grace in the schools, and many of the children gave promise of true conversion to God. Thirty-four were enabled to forsake idolatry, and obtained salvation through the Lord Jesus Christ; but not so large a proportion of these were of the female sex as on the previous occasions. There were, however, two girls and a few women who confessed Christ, and were baptized in His name.

Another deep sorrow in due time succeeded this joy, the death of her eldest son—a heavy stroke, which well-nigh prostrated her; and though she was sustained by Him who inflicted it, she was from this time evidently ripening for her better home. The last night of the year 1832 was spent in prayer with the brethren, and all realised in a lively manner the uncertainty of life through the opening year. If uncommon fitness for heaven were observed in any, it was in Mrs Winslow, whose lamp was indeed trimmed, and her light burning; but no one, perhaps, except herself, heard the voice, "The Master is come, and calleth for thee."

In expectation of her confinement, concerning the issue of which she was, for no apparent reason, uncommonly doubtful, she made her preparations much as she would have done had she known that she would be unable at last to bid any one farewell. All the concerns of the boarding-school, as well as the affairs of her household, and of the station as far as under her management, were arranged in the most careful manner, and written directions left concerning them. There was also a paper of hints relating to her children, and a farewell letter to her husband.

Nor was her soul neglected. She had laid up fresh provision for passing over Jordan. Her affliction, by weaning her from the world, by making the Bible and a throne of grace more precious, by causing her to look to a compassionate Saviour with more steady faith, and to appropriate to herself more than ever before the precious promises of His Word, so changed the current of her religious feelings, and so carried them upward, that she often spoke of them as entirely new.

On Sunday, January 13th, 1833, though able to attend divine service twice, she was evidently ill; and during the ensuing night, after severe pain, succeeded by quiet sleep, she resigned her spirit gently and peacefully into her Redeemer's hands, and went to receive joy for all her sorrow in the presence of her Lord.

Shall we add some paragraphs to this brief notice, which will show that those who have entered into Mrs Winslow's labours have reaped in joy the fruit which has been gathered from her early sowing in tears.

A year or two ago, it could be said of this part of the mission-field, that one native convert had been for forty years a mother in Israel, and her eldest daughter, baptized into the same Spirit, is the wife of a venerable pastor, a man full of years and of graces.

In the congregation to which he ministers you are introduced to entire families, including every female; and they may be seen walking in groups to the house of God, attired in the most graceful costume, their jackets and muslin head-dresses beautifully embroidered by themselves—an art learned in the mission-school. The effect of their training appears in their persons, manners, homes, children, and servants. An encouraging picture this of Christian life in the midst of still heathen Jaffnapatam, and one which manifests the blessing that has been given to female missionary labour.

MRS MARY ANNE WILSON.

[Born 1784. Died 1868, aged 84. A missionary in India twenty-three years.]

So many incidental notices of Mrs Wilson's Indian career have been necessarily introduced into our sketches of female work in Bengal, that this special memoir will pass over much we should otherwise bring out.

She was truly a shining light in the darkest night of India's still dark land, and even a passing allusion to her earlier days will be interesting to those whose hearts are alive to missionary details. The remarkable incidents in her career might well form an important volume in the history of female missions, but it is only to the main facts that we must allow ourselves to refer.

No notice of the birth or parentage of Mary Anne Cooke is accessible to us. She first appears upon the scene as an accomplished governess in the family of the Earl of Mulgrave, where she won the love of pupils, who, after following her with unabated interest through her twenty-three years of foreign service, felt it their joy and privilege to minister to her comfort and happiness in her declining days, to stand by her dying bed, listen to her last words, and receive her expiring breath.

Miss Cooke's thoughts were first directed to India and its suffering women by an appeal to the ladies of Liverpool, addressed to them by the Rev. W. Ward of Serampur. The work of their evangelisation appeared in those days to present difficulties almost insurmountable to the eye of sense. But what cannot prayer, pains, and perseverance do even in such cases; and it is evident from the blessing that followed, that the day of grace for India's women was dawning, and God had prepared a choice and chosen instrument to begin the work in Miss Cooke.

Home ties were broken, and in 1821, at the age of thirty-seven, the voyage was made to the land of her adoption in company with an eminent missionary, the Rev. John Mack, whose views being kindred to her own, they strengthened each other in their noble purpose. Two years later Mary Bird followed.

Having arrived in Calcutta, Miss Cooke's first work was to master the Bengali language; and this acquired, sufficiently to communicate simple ideas, she went into the native bazaars and attracted the children around her, as she sat down outside a mat hut knitting and reading. The mothers followed, and she soon obtained the consent of many to the instruction of their little girls. An anecdote strikingly illustrative of the way in which God works when His plans are ripening for the accomplishment of certain purposes, is related in a previous chapter; so with this general allusion to the first stage of Miss Cooke's labours we pass on to mention her union with a missionary of the Church Missionary Society, the Rev. Mr Wilson, a union which was formed with the full understanding that no interruption should in consequence occur to *her* special branch of work.

The success which attended her efforts to form a number of girls' schools has been particularised in the history. There was at that time all the attraction of novelty in this department, and it seemed to promise very extensive results; so that, encouraged by a donation from a native gentleman, Mrs Wilson proceeded to raise funds for the erection of a large central building in the midst of the native town of Calcutta, and on the 1st April 1828 she took possession of her new home. The various small and scattered schools were gradually concentrated and brought to this spot, till the daily attendance numbered three hundred children. In December of the same year the first examination was held under this new roof.

Mr Wilson was a man eminently calculated to support and assist his wife in her labours; but it became necessary for him to visit England on missionary business, after their plans had thus far prospered, and feeling how important her presence was at this stage of progress, she consented to let him embark alone.

A sudden and short illness terminated his life soon after the voyage began, and she was again left a solitary worker. The blow prostrated her for a time, and she sought a change by visiting missionary stations in the country, but with her heart bent on her beloved work. As she passed from place to place, she had many opportunities of awakening and deepening an interest in India's poor daughters among those she met, stimulating them to exertion by her loving, earnest words.

The testimony of one well known among our Indian missionaries, the Rev. J. J. Weitbrecht, refers to her at this period :—

"We received a visit from Mrs Wilson, a noble woman with few equals, entirely devoted to the Lord's work among the heathen, creating a spirit of joy and gladness wherever she goes. She examined the female schools scattered through the villages, and passed on to Bancura, where her zeal and love led her to try and benefit all classes. She encouraged the ladies there to interest themselves for the women, as those at Burdwan were doing. A most profitable Sabbath was past; conversation on God's Word drew from Mrs Wilson remarks so striking, that increased desire to follow Jesus was aroused, and she started in the evening leaving a delightful impression behind her."

At Kishnaghur, another missionary station, she found fifty girls in the school, thirty of whom were Brahmans; for Christian ladies there had already been led to make zealous efforts for their enthralled sisters, and such success as was unparalleled then, though happily no longer uncommon, had followed.

The general influence Mrs Wilson had by this time obtained was remarkable. Her wisdom and discretion, her calm and genial temper, her deep but cheerful piety, and her eight years' experience, together with her extremely practical power, enabling her to use every talent effectively, all combined to attract to her a rare measure of confidence and affection. Her qualifications for her special sphere were indeed very manifest.

To begin the work of elevating the females of India from their degraded condition, one was wanted who could combine with systematic but silent perseverance the meekness of wisdom; one who should unite the tender, loving heart of an ordinary mother, with the firmness, ability, and strength of a mother in Israel. Mrs W. possessed all these qualities. She had great sagacity, with intense though quiet enthusiasm; she had deep sympathy, unfailing love, deadness to the world, discretion of purpose, entire consecration of heart, great largeness of mind, command of temper, and a deep acquaintance both with the heart of man and the Word of God.

One who knew her well, and worked with her, says—"Love to Jesus as her Saviour, and desire to make Him known to others, was the marked feature and predominating thought of her heart, to which every wish and plan was subjected; and this gave her that single eye, that purity of thought, that abhorrence of evil, that devotion of spirit, that unflinching self-denial, which enabled her in an unusual degree to exemplify the divine charity which 'suffereth long and is kind, seeketh not her own, thinketh no evil, beareth all things, believeth all things, hopeth all things, endureth all things.'"

She possessed not only excellent administrative power, but the art of making others useful—in fact, of creating instrumentality for work; and in her special mission this was one great reason of her success. Her natural cheerfulness abounded, and though of deep and strong affection and sensitive to suffering, both in herself and others, a simple, child-like faith supplied her hourly with the spirit of thanksgiving and praise. This buoyancy of the natural and spiritual life, sustained by the constant study of God's Word and prayer, enabled her to undertake great things for her beloved Lord and Master, never realising a difficulty that could not be overcome in His strength, or a suffering too hard to sustain with His support.

A sketch of the impression made by a visit to Mrs Wilson, upon a newly-arrived female worker, in those days, may give the reader a more lively idea of her power than the foregoing description of her character :—

"It was in the year 1833, on one of those cool, bright mornings peculiar to the month of January in Calcutta, that I was set down in a palanquin at the entrance of a house in Cornwallis Square, the centre of the native city. This house was outwardly one of those imposing-looking buildings which give to Calcutta the name of the City of Palaces. It had, however, been prepared for anything rather than a royal residence, as I soon perceived on my entrance, for the floors of the large matted halls, as well as those of the spacious verandahs, were covered with circles of little native girls, distinguished more by their dirty, uncouth appearance, than by any outward attraction.

But there was a lady standing among these

hundreds of swarthy little ones to whom they were objects of the deepest interest; and I at once perceived, as she began to speak of them, and took me round and introduced me more nearly to them, that her heart was drawn out in most intense sympathy towards them; and I can, at this distance of time, recall in a lively way the very tones of her voice, as she communicated to me various details of her work.

This lady was Mrs Wilson, the chief pioneer of female education in Bengal—not the first in order of time, but the one who gave it its greatest impetus. She was a noble woman, genial, kind, large-hearted, and full of Christian love. Native gentlemen who had helped her in building this house, styled her, in their oriental phraseology, a diamond, a gem, and such-like honourable titles; and certain it is, that she was in very truth peerless among her fellows.

Mrs Wilson, as already indicated, had left her native country in her best years, to go forth in the hope of raising the degraded daughters of India from their débased condition, by teaching them not only to read, but to know the Saviour whose love gave her power to make this sacrifice—a far greater one at that time than now. She had, therefore, at the period of my visit, been some twelve years in the country, and most faithfully had she redeemed her trust during those years.

It is very pleasant even now to recollect how the heart warmed to her and her work as she led me from class to class, and told me something of her early efforts and difficulties. She related how she had tried little day-schools in various parts of Calcutta; how she had gone from place to place visiting and examining them day by day; how at length some Hindu Babus had been stirred up, by observing these things, to offer a handsome sum of money that a central house might be erected where all her pupils might be gathered around her together.

"And now you see them before you," she said, "to the number of three hundred;" and she proceeded to point out the classes who had advanced so far as to be able to read St John's Gospel fluently, and I heard them. "When I bring them thus far," she said, "I bless God;" and then she told me of one dear girl, who had found Jesus, of whom that Gospel is so full, and who had become a happy, useful Christian wife and mother, and a teacher too, in the service of a neighbouring missionary. These were the days of first-fruits, rare and scanty, but an earnest of future blessings, for which we early labourers had to wait and pray."

After some years spend at this central school, Mrs Wilson conceived the idea of a female orphanage, for which she obtained support entirely through her personal influence. This building rises on the banks of the Ganges, and refreshes the eye in passing up its stream midway between Calcutta and Barrackpur. The name of the native village is Agurparah, and it remains to this present day a centre of extensive evangelistic work. Under the auspices of Mrs Wilson there was built not only an orphanage, but a church adjacent to it, and a pretty simple parsonage, for the residence of the missionary in charge. Mrs Wilson herself resided in the orphanage.

An old missionary, the Rev. M. Wilkinson, has left a touching description of a visit he paid to this refuge with his wife, probably about the year 1840.

"We were met," he writes, "on our arrival by the kind owner of the house, who with her accustomed Christian cordiality soon initiated us into the routine of her daily operations, and the varied arrangements of her important and interesting institution. Morning school had just ended as we arrived, and as we were no strangers to Mrs Wilson's little flock, many cordial greetings passed between us and them.

"We soon had the pleasure of seeing the dear children at their morning meal, seated on the floor in their usual native mode, around three sides of a long room. One of the eldest asked the blessing of the Christian's God upon the food He had given, and praised Him for it when the simple meal was done.

"It was a lovely sight to behold so many Indian females so cared for and so blessed, more especially when the mind glanced at what their condition might have been had not this refuge been opened for them —slaves—outcasts—lost for time and for eternity. No approach to European manners, save the important one alluded to, and that of extreme cleanliness, was observable in their meal; for it is Mrs Wilson's wise resolve to bring up these children in a manner which will render them fitted for the stations they may be called upon to fill. Indeed, all here bore the stamp of consistent practical piety.

"After dinner many of the children assembled and read the Scriptures in English, translating them into Bengali as they proceeded, in a way which clearly proved their understanding of the sacred truths they read. They also sang several English hymns to English tunes very sweetly. One large and airy schoolroom contained many classes busily employed in reading the Scriptures in Bengali, English, &c., while in another twelve or fourteen were engaged in woolwork, which they have learned to do most beautifully.

"Distant from the contamination of the city, and far from its noise and tumult, this invaluable institution is working its important way, its inmates being, as much as possible, independent of all without its walls; for the children are taught to labour for themselves and those about them, and their efforts are found amply sufficient for the proper discharge of the domestic duties of the Refuge, thus dispensing with that most fertile source of vice in India—heathen servants.

"The situation of the Refuge is interesting. Standing as it does on the bank of an extensive reach, it affords a lovely prospect of the majestic flood as it rolls on its way, spotted with barks of all descriptions, not the less beautiful to a European eye because they are rudely constructed. To us the air was balm, and seemed to bring health and strength on its wings as it swept over the mighty river; nor were our souls untouched, for all things seemed to say, 'Christian, thy God is here.' Pray, ye that love the Lord Jesus, that the blessing of Jehovah may abundantly rest on this oasis in this vast desert of idolatry, that many may be the palm-trees that shall flourish there."

After some years given to this interesting sphere of missionary labour, Mrs Wilson's views altered on some important points, and it was deemed desirable that she should retire from her loved work. It was deeply lamented by her fellow-workers that anything should withdraw her from the land to which she had consecrated her life. But the Lord whom she loved might have foreseen her as liable to be lifted up with pride or to be honoured with undue honour, and so permitted the concurrence of circumstances which led to her withdrawal, not only from Agurpara, but from India, ere any portion of the lustre of her example had been dimmed, or her own deep spirituality and devotion had been marred.

Part of the remaining twenty-three years of her pilgrimage were spent in Syria, where she went to establish an Arabic female school; and part in Italy, where she laboured in the Gospel before the days of freedom. The latest part of her long life was passed in England, laid aside from regular service, yet no cumberer of the ground. Her bright and active spirit never seemed to fail; and at the age of eighty-four she came to her end, as a shock of corn fully ripe cometh in its season.

Her last words were, "Jesus—happy;" and in the maturity of experience, and the full assurance of faith and hope, she entered into the joy of her Lord.

"Blessed are the dead who die in the Lord: they

rest from their labours, and their works do follow them."

The contrast between *Mary Anne Wilson* and *Mary Bird* is striking. The one, full of physical, practical, and spiritual power, worked long and accomplished much. The other, feeble in body though strong in spirit, was honoured to do individually and noiselessly an important work, and to prepare the way for those who succeeded her in an eminent though almost unperceived and unrecognised way. The one was much honoured of man; the other honoured with many honours as a good and faithful servant by Him who summoned her in the midst of her days and of her usefulness to enter into His joy. They lived and prayed for each other on earth; they now taste that communion which will never be marred by disappointment or interrupted by death.

MARY BIRD.

[Born 1789. Died 1833. 1823–1833, ten years in India.]

AMONG those who must be reckoned as eminent female missionaries, Mary Bird stands conspicuous, both for the amount of work she accomplished, and the early period at which she entered the field. She was an English lady of good birth, whose brother occupied a high position in the service of the East India Company.

The antecedents of this lady's life had prepared

her in a remarkable manner for missionary service. The child of godly parents, carefully trained in the way of holiness by a pious mother, and highly educated in all useful knowledge and accomplishments, she was led, through long illness in early life, to decide for Christ, and to dedicate the powers of a very superior natural character to the service of this divine Master.

Having in those youthful days, when impressions are so deeply made, visited New York, she greatly profited by the friendship of a venerable Christian lady, Mrs Isabella Graham, whose philanthropic labours were so great a blessing to that city. *Her* conversation and general influence powerfully helped to mature the Christian character of Mary Bird.

While yet a young woman, she was perseveringly diligent in labours among rich and poor, as opportunity opened in either direction; and the God whom she loved and served gave a rich blessing to her efforts, and permitted her the joy of seeing many souls united to Christ through her instructions and winning persuasiveness.

In 1823 a call from a beloved brother in India led her to that country, moved not only by the hope of ministering to his comfort and enjoyment, but with the earnest longing to carry the message of Jesus' love to the benighted women of that dark land. In 1823, at the age of thirty-four, Mary Bird entered courageously on an entirely fresh sphere of life and service for the great Master, undaunted by the difficulties of a new and strange language.

Her brother's station was Gorruckpur, about five hundred miles north-west of Calcutta, the chief town in a retired district on the borders of a dense forest nearly twenty-four miles in depth. Here she at once studied and acquired the native language, becoming so familiar with it as to superintend a school for boys, to organise one for girls, and to prepare books in the vernacular for the use of her pupils.

Her brother's position as judge gave her an influence which she used in overcoming the prejudices of the people so far as to make her attempt at female education a success, an almost unknown circumstance in those days in an isolated station. Lovingly and prayerfully she pursued her daily course, not simply teaching to read, but trying to win the souls of the little ones for Jesus. Nor did she labour in vain.

After a few years' service, circumstances led Mary Bird to Calcutta. She could then have returned to England, as her family earnestly desired, but her heart burned far too warmly towards her Hindu sisters to permit her to forsake them; and with a courage which those only who knew the sensitiveness of her nature could estimate, she at once entered on a wide and fruitful sphere of labour in that city.

No power but that of love could thus have animated a feeble, delicate, and timid woman, acutely alive to the opinions of those among whom she lived, through evil and through good report. The path she marked out for herself, new, and hitherto untrodden, was to visit at their homes numerous females descended from European fathers and native mothers, with whom Calcutta then abounded, who spoke Hindustani, but were totally unable to benefit by instruction in English, or indeed to *read* any language at all.

To these neglected ones Mary Bird became a ministering spirit, visiting them in their homes, and inducing them to assemble in classes at her own dwelling, so that soon a group of these despised young girls were seen clustering around her, drinking in from her lips the life-giving truth of salvation through Jesus, which to many became glad tidings of great joy.

Her next attempt was to introduce herself to the purely native women in the zenanas. Many rebuffs did she meet, but she *did* often succeed in gaining admittance into the innermost apartment, where she was listened to by its inmates, if not at first with pleasure, with most eager curiosity.

She appeared to these poor women as one bringing tidings from the world, which was to them like a distant land; and when trying to explain to them some familiar subject, they would interrupt her with childish questions suggested by it to their minds. She was often moved to smile, and tell them they must excuse her, for she could not just then wait to explain how the large ships which they had heard of were as high as the house, why they did not sink in the water, and how they knew their way when there was no coast to be seen. And then they would rejoin, "This English lady has a very pleasing way; we wish she would come often, and tell us how many sisters and brothers she has, and why she is not married," &c.

After such digressions it would be long before she could get them all serious and silent again; but her love to their souls gave her patience with them, and prayer to her Father in heaven gave her supplies of grace and strength to persevere in her efforts for them. And she had her reward, for she was blessed in many cases, which will prove her crown of rejoicing in the day when she will be numbered among those who, having turned many to righteousness, shall shine as the stars for ever and ever. These incipient labours of Mary Bird in what is now well known as zenana visitation, had their indirect effect in preparing the way for future efforts, and their direct one in the communication of light and life to some whose seclusion in the recesses of the zenana prevented its rays from penetrating beyond zenana walls in those deeply-prejudiced days.

She devoted Thursday evening in every week to the girls before alluded to, who came to her own residence. By degrees the number increased, and for two years they were joined in the afternoons of Sundays by a few native converts, under the instruction of a Christian moulvi, who assisted by reading the prayers and exposition of Scripture which Mary Bird had previously prepared. At the time of her death there were no less than fifty-five girls who were thus receiving instruction in the way of eternal life.

Her method of communicating knowledge was so happy, that she was requested by several of the ladies conducting schools in Calcutta to devote some time each week to imparting religious instruction to their pupils. This she most readily did, and for the same purpose she visited the orphan school at Alipur.* She also established a Bible-class, consisting of about thirty young girls, who regularly assembled every Monday evening.

She afforded her most cordial assistance in forming a Sunday-school at the Free School Church, and once a week instructed a class of native boys under the care of the Christian moulvi in geography.

During this time her labours in English and Hindustani composition did not cease. Besides her "Commentary on the Book of Genesis," well calculated for the improvement of families and schools, she published, both in English and Hindustani, "England Delineated," and fitted several valuable school-books for more general use in India. She completed the "Outline of Ancient History," and translated the whole of it into Hindustani.

She finished a tract on the Ten Commandments, which had been commenced at Gorruckpur, besides several smaller tracts. She translated also a small work on geography of her own composition, a valuable treatise on astronomy, with illustrative plates, and was engaged on a "History of England," which she had brought down to the reign of William II., when she died. In translating the work on astronomy she encountered many mathematical difficulties which were new to her; but till she fully under-

* An institution near Calcutta for the education and training of the daughters of officers who married Eurasians, and died in India.

stood them, she did not give up the study, or attempt to continue the translation.

As a remarkable instance of this, we may mention that, having to explain the computation of the distance of the earth from the sun, she was not satisfied till she had made herself mistress of the mathematical demonstration of doing so by the transit of Venus, for the purpose of inserting it in her translation.

Her peculiarly bright and happy nature, winning love from all around her, helped her through the daily routine of what might seem irksome employment.

Thus were the powers and gifts of this interesting woman used simply and entirely for the glory of Him to whom she had dedicated her life, though her delicacy, and a distressing lameness, the result of an accident in early youth, might have caused her to shrink from the fatigue and discomfort incident on such a sphere; but no one of those things moved her, nor did she count her life dear unto herself, so that she might finish her course with joy in the ministry which she had received of the Lord Jesus.

That course was, alas! fast drawing to a close. The evening before her death she passed at the Kidderpur Orphan School, apparently in perfect health, or as well as could be during the extreme heat of the weather. At night she felt indisposed, but delayed sending for medical aid till morning. It then became evident that an attack of cholera was upon her, the messenger sent to summon her to receive the reward of the good and faithful servant.

After a few hours of patient suffering, this beloved of the Lord went to dwell in safety by Him, resting from her labours, while her works do follow her. The shortness of her illness, and extreme prostration, prevented any expression of feeling in the prospect of death; but when, sixteen months before, she had been delivered from a great danger, she exclaimed, "Others will say what an escape I have had, but I cannot help thinking how pleasant it had been to have joined the Church of the firstborn, and have done for ever with the perplexities and the trials of this evil world;" and only ten days before, she had said, on taking leave of a friend, "I cannot think of England, and would not wish to, while health continues and work abounds, and while, undeserving as I am, refreshings from on high, and ardent longings to be with Christ, and to live for Him only, are so graciously granted me."

Mrs Wilson stood beside her dying bed, and told her there was little hope of her recovery; and soon after, on the 29th of May, her birthday both in an earthly and heavenly sense, her redeemed spirit was with Jesus in Paradise, and she saw her living Saviour face to face.

Crowds of natives showed the love they felt towards her by attending her funeral.

Though so deeply attached to her home circle, she cheerfully left ease to endure toil, forsook the company of beloved friends for the privilege of conveying salvation to India's dark daughters; and she now speaks from her grave on the banks of the Ganges to those left behind, bidding them take up the work she has laid down, and win for themselves the crown which has been placed on her brow. "Be thou faithful unto death, and I will give thee a crown of life."

MARGARET WILSON.

[Born 1795. Died 1845. Laboured seven years.]

WILL our readers now accompany us to another part of the vast continent of India, and let us introduce them to the lady who was honoured of God, not quite to *commence*, but to consolidate and enlarge the work of native female education in Bombay. She was, as will be seen in the narrative, a well-prepared and polished instrument; and though her career was a comparatively brief one, a vast amount of much-blessed work was crowded into these few years, and a spirit infused into that work of which it has never lost the impress.

Margaret Bayne, the eldest daughter of a very pious minister of Christ in Scotland, was born at Greenock, November 5th, 1795. She was one of those happy children who are sanctified from their very birth, and could remember no period of her life when not conscious of the gracious working of the Holy Spirit within her. The death of her pious mother, when she was thirteen, powerfully tended to influence the solemn working of her spirit; and though naturally animated, she became at that time quite absorbed in the contemplation of holy things, so that secret and social prayer, meditation and attendance at public worship, were her meat and drink.

This early and remarkable dedication of all her powers to God prepared her, two years later, to take a mother's place in the family, and a younger sister writes, "Every day seemed to increase our love and admiration of her, and with some of the veneration due to a parent, we felt joyous, happy, and unconstrained under her care."

But the responsibility of her charge pressed deeply on her spirit, and many a prayer did she offer, many a tear did she shed on their account. Often would she retire, with one after another of these younger children, to instruct, to entreat, and to pray with them; and God gave her the desire of her heart. To one brother in particular her efforts were early blessed.

After her sisters were placed at school, she devoted her time to the cultivation of her own mind, reading much and deeply on almost every subject, and fascinating her companions by her mental power. Thus better fitted for the charge, she resumed the care of her sisters' education, and in union with them taught a Sabbath-school with much affectionate faithfulness, and used her many gifts in other Christian work.

She consented to become the wife of a missionary, the Rev. John Wilson, in 1827, and the beginning of the year 1829 found her in India. "It is impossible," wrote she, "to describe the deathlike cessation of feeling which ensued when my heart told me I was severed from you, my beloved, my dearest sisters, perhaps for ever! But instead of dwelling on this, let us turn to the glorious realities of that state where there is no more sorrow, no more parting pangs."

From a worker so equipped as Mrs Wilson, we naturally look for corresponding results. Nor are we disappointed; for had she then known that only seven years of missionary life were allotted her, she could not have commenced her labours more promptly and vigorously.

It is true that before she reached Bombay girls' schools were in operation, under the superintendence of Mrs Stevenson, who had laboured diligently in this department; but this lady was soon removed to Puna, where she successfully continued her zealous efforts; and the impulse needed for the consolidation, continuance, and enlargement of the work at Bombay was given by the timely arrival of Mrs Wilson. There were great obstacles to be overcome here, as elsewhere; but her spirit was not to be daunted by opposition, and before she had been many months in India she could count fifty-three scholars; and in a few months more, six girls' schools in active operation, with a hundred and twenty pupils. Till the middle of 1831, when she took a long tour with her husband, the health of both having suffered, she worked in these schools with untiring energy and perseverance, and with much encouragement.

The seclusion of the higher classes of women on the western side of India is not nearly so complete as in the valley of the Ganges, where two of those female missionaries whose memoirs we have given were located. The Mahratta population are far less careful on this point than their Eastern brethren in Bengal and North-West India, so that *their* prejudices arise chiefly from their apathy and their persuasion of the uselessness of teaching *women.* Mrs Wilson had to combat these views; and this done successfully, the work went rapidly forward.

In 1832 Mrs Wilson's schools contained a hundred and seventy-six girls of the poorest and humblest description. She assembled them weekly in her own house, and sought, by a strict examination, and by affectionate exhortation, to fix in their understandings, and impress on their hearts, the truths with which they were becoming familiar.

The most destitute class, whose poverty would not allow them to send their children for instruction without that support which they earned by going messages, carrying small loads, or doing other petty services, also attracted her particular attention; and encouraged by the promise of funds, and co-operation from Christian ladies at Bombay, she resolved to found a school for their express benefit, in which what was needed to secure their attendance should be freely afforded.

Great difficulties were experienced in carrying the design into effect; but care in explaining to the natives the objects in view, the visible comfort of the few girls who were at first admitted, and prayer and perseverance, ere long prevailed. The Institution, which was the first of its kind in this part of India, was remarkably blessed, and several of its scholars became the first-fruits unto Christ of female education in Bombay.

Having accomplished her aim in regard to the day-schools, Mrs Wilson formed an orphanage and boarding-school, and writes in reference to it and other work—"I take the entire superintendence of the school, and consider this affords me a most valuable opportunity of conveying a knowledge of divine truth to the females of India. I feel that every increase of occupation brings with it an increase of happiness; and I see in this arrangement a wonderful illustration of the goodness of God. Had I contemplated at a distance the number and variety of duties which now devolve upon me, I should have been appalled at the prospect; but instead of lessening, they greatly add to my enjoyment."

Mr Wilson's health needing change at this time, his wife remained behind superintending the arduous duties of the mission with a vigour and application of which few indeed could be capable.

But this earnest and zealous worker in her Master's vineyard had, with all her fellow-labourers, to make the experience of sore and heavy chastening; and while thus "in labours very abundant," she received a message from Scotland of most painful bereavement. Two of those sisters so dear to her heart were drowned while bathing; and just after, her own little son of eighteen months was transferred from her arms to those of his Saviour.

These bereavements, following some severe trials in her work, greatly prostrated her physically; yet she rose above them in spirit, and accompanied her husband in a long missionary tour; but serious illness supervened, and she was ordered to Europe.

Mr Wilson's feeble health, and her own intense interest in the people over whom her heart yearned, decided her to remain and labour on, simply moving for awhile to a retired spot for rest and change. Here, in the solitude and peace of the place, she seemed to have more of spiritual enjoyment than she had ever experienced before. Nor was her time unemployed, for she had not been there many days, when, finding the pain in her side easier, she went on Sunday to instruct the native women.

"I had no sooner sat down," she writes, "than I got a large congregation—all our own servants, and a number of other people. I began to shake when I saw them arrayed before me; but when I remembered that they were immortal beings, and knew not the precious gospel, I went on, forgetful of language, logic, and even of good pronunciation."

There was in July of this year (1833) much religious excitement among the natives, for the earnest efforts of the missionaries had begun to tell. There were also discouraging and depressing orders to diminish work received from home; but Mrs Wilson disregarded them, and went on in the even tenor of her way, writing—"My mission-schools are doing well: and I feel that we have a work of faith and a labour of love, and that we must not give it up in despair."

The last sentence is with reference to the bazaar

school, many of the little girls of which, instead of devoting their time to their studies, had often to go and cut grass for the bazaar. Their relatives employed them in this way while they were able to obtain any money by their work. The school was thus emptied, and at a standstill. In January 1834, however, the schools contained upwards of two hundred girls, and were never in a more promising state.

Mrs Wilson's progress in Marathi and Hindustani, the principal languages spoken in Bombay, had for several years enabled her to communicate verbal instruction to the old and to the young with fluency and power, and her daily instructions in them continued for hours, whenever her strength would permit—and even when many would have thought it expended, were such as to awaken the admiration of all who witnessed them.

Before the conclusion of 1833 she became exceedingly desirous to use her pen for the benefit of natives in a more satisfactory manner than she had yet done, by writing occasional short pieces. The first object to which she directed her attention was the preparation, in Marathi, of an abridgment of a large part of Rollin's "Ancient History," for the use of her schools, and native youth in general. After some months' application she completed it as far as the accounts of the Egyptians, Babylonians, Assyrians, Medes, Persians, and Athenians were concerned; and she kept her manuscript beside her for a future revision, which she had nearly completed before she was called to rest from her labours.

The disadvantages under which converts from Hinduism labour, with regard to some of the means of grace, being at that time very great, sympathy with their difficulties led her to resolve to prepare for them a series of devotional exercises, calculated by their simplicity for the native mind. In this important work she made considerable progress.

Another object on which she greatly set her heart was a review, intended for the use of the children of her schools, of the history of the Church, and a particular narrative of the labours and sufferings of its most distinguished members, in the profession and propagation of the truth. Such a work, she thought, would not only prove interesting and instructive to them, but encourage them to avow the convictions which many of them felt respecting the vanity and guilt of idolatry, and the suitableness to their circumstances of the gospel of Jesus. She made considerable preparations for its execution, and she wrote out some letters which were to introduce the subject to her readers.

But in May 1834, her gradually-advancing weakness induced the feeling that her labours and warfare on earth, though not less abundant than at any period of her missionary career, were speedily drawing to a close. "Of late," she writes, "I have experienced considerable prostration of strength, and have had a bad cough and pain in my side; I sometimes feel that my days on earth *cannot* be many. These symptoms of weakness and dissolution are messengers of love. They are sent to warn us against seeking repose and security in a world of shadows. They teach us the value of Christ's triumph over death and the grave, and they lead us to direct our thoughts and bend our steps heavenward."

All her letters from this period bore this impression. In one to her sisters she reviewed with feelings of intensest gratitude to God, and with unlimited confidence in His wisdom, faithfulness, and grace, the various afflictions with which she had been visited during her pilgrim journey. She literally, under heaven-born influences, "gloried in tribulations," and anticipated their happiest issue. Under a deep sense of unworthiness, and sighing for deliverance, she hailed the speedy approach of that time when her ransomed soul would exult in the unbounded freedom of its purified nature.

At this period her daily occupations consisted of two hours in study, preparatory to future usefulness, and the same amount of time in writing for the press in the native languages, associating her literary labours with earnest efforts for the conversion of those who were aiding her; and three hours daily did she spend in a spirit of holy importunity among the native children of her schools. She went day after day a distance of three miles, walking through several narrow streets into which her vehicle could not enter, visiting one of the Portuguese schools of the mission, instructing several families of Europeans, who unhappily made the name of Christ a reproach to the heathen; and then returning to her home, the evening was spent in her family, instructing her children, and writing letters to her friends in Scotland and elsewhere.

At the close of the year she accompanied Mr Wilson to Surat, journeying in extreme weakness, but in hope of thereby lengthening out for a little longer her days of sweet service for the Master she loved so well. Her journal, kept on this tour, is very touching, manifesting her deep spirituality and perfect peace, her intense compassion for the multitudes, and her zealous efforts to unfold to those she could reach—and she did reach a large number—the love and infinite grace of Jesus.

In it we trace the holy ardour of her Christian affections, the maturity of her Christian experience, and her great delight in prayer and divine worship, combined with admiration of the beauty and grandeur of God's works around her, indicating the glory of His character, and suggestive of what awaited her in the better, brighter home she was rapidly nearing.

The little strength gained on this journey soon faded away in the hot weather and the routine of work, so that she writes—"I lately thought my day was well-nigh ended, but the Lord spares me yet. It is a general relaxation of the system, and I have to abstain from much mental effort,—a great trial, as I had undertaken the translation of several works; but our times are in the Lord's hands. I am now able to do a little in the schools, but have to be cautious.* The traces of sin are seen in everything here; it is a land of darkness and exile, making us

* The day-schools alone contained, in 1840, 519 pupils.

long for *home.* Oh for the eye of faith, to catch a glimpse of the purity and bliss of that home, and to walk here as pilgrims and strangers!"

In March 1835, a sentence, "worse than death" to her, was pronounced: she must leave India.

It was not executed, and her strong desire to die among the people to whose spiritual welfare she had dedicated her life was granted. She told her doctor and her husband that she had long looked forward to her death, and had "her house in order." On the day following she laid her down to die.

During the short period of confinement to her couch her interest in her work was still lively, and she gave minute directions about the publication of her Marathi translations and compositions, some papers which she wished to appear in the *Oriental Christian Spectator*, and the disposal of her female schools. To all the children who had been under her care, she requested that her dying testimony should be conveyed, as to the power and glory of the gospel which she had taught them. To some of them, whose hearts God had touched, and who after her death were admitted into the Christian Church, she left special messages. All the converts of the mission she particularly mentioned, begging that her most faithful and affectionate counsel should be conveyed to them.

She said that on looking back on her intercourse with the natives, and her efforts for their instruction and improvement, she could not much blame herself for *indolence*, but that she had great reason to lament her impatience and unbelief. "India," she exclaimed, "is dark, dark, but speedily will be light; God will most assuredly fulfil His promises, and give the heathen to His Son for an inheritance, and the uttermost parts of the earth for a possession."*

In the silence of midnight, when she thought no human eye was upon her, and no human ear within the compass of her voice, and with the expectation of immediately entering into the eternal world, she repeated aloud the whole of that beautiful hymn, "The hour of my departure's come," with an earnestness never to be forgotten by some who heard her.

The Bible, infinitely precious to her through life, was still the source of delight and joy. Even when under the delirium of disease, she called upon her friends repeatedly to bring her the Word of God. After addressing the Saviour in earnest prayer, one evening when she thought herself dying, she repeated aloud a portion of the Song of Solomon—"I sat down under His shadow with great delight, and His fruit was sweet to my taste." "Read to me," she would say, "the 43d chapter of Isaiah; I like to hear the promise, 'When thou passest through the waters, I will be with thee; and through the rivers, they shall not overflow thee,'" &c.

The two last chapters of the Revelation afforded her the greatest delight. After hearing them she exclaimed, "How glorious is this description of heaven!" On hearing the 23d Psalm, she said,

* Only four years after her death, in 1849, the first Parsi schools were opened in Bombay, which gave a fresh impetus to female education in general in that part of India.

"How I can, from the heart, adopt *every word* of that Psalm." The 46th, which Luther and Melancthon used to sing in their troubles, she also found very sustaining.

During her illness, she was occupied in prayer whenever left alone. Her prayers for her children were frequent, and fervent beyond conception. She agonised with God for their sanctification and dedication for work in India. When informed of the birthday of one of them, she, in the most solemn manner, dictated a letter which she wished might be sent to him; and having written, "Your own devoted mother, Margaret Wilson," with her own hand, she laid down the pen, never more to take it up, and said, "Now I am ready to die."

When she realised death near, she said, "The Lord is hearing my prayers; oh, how gracious He is to my soul!" Her anticipations of eternal glory were expressed in language the most beautiful and affecting. "To-morrow's sun," she exclaimed, "will rise—though not upon me. But I shall behold *Him* who is as the sun shining forth in his strength—even the Sun of Righteousness, and I shall be ravished by His infinite glory. He will never go down upon my soul. Thanks be to God, who giveth us the victory through our Lord Jesus Christ." Never, during the whole of her illness, did she express the slightest doubt of her acceptance in Christ.

On one occasion she exclaimed, "I cannot look steadily—I cannot look steadily; it is the glory sparkling behind the cloud which overpowers me. But soon shall it all burst forth upon my soul, and I shall be enabled to bear it, and to drink up its beams." Nothing during the three days preceding her death interfered with the fullest exercise of her spiritual affections, or disturbed the accuracy of her judgment of divine things. When she thought herself surrounded by friends who were distant from her, she addressed them with a tenderness and kindness which strikingly showed the strength of her attachment. Even in the languages of India she would converse on the divine faithfulness and grace.

On the last morning she recognised the kind friends who were around her bed, mentioned their names, and followed with them several psalms, into the devotion of which she seemed fully to enter. A few hours later, on Sunday, April 19th, 1845, her soul winged its flight to that glorious abode where Jesus lives and reigns, and where she will reign with Him.

"Absent from flesh! O blissful thought!
What joys unknown this moment brings!
Freed from the mischiefs sin has wrought,
From pains and fears, and all their springs.

"Absent from flesh! illustrious day,
Surprising scene, triumphant stroke
That rends the prison of my clay,
And I can feel my fetters broke!

"Absent from flesh! then rise, my soul,
Where feet nor wings could ever climb;
Beyond the heavens, where planets roll,
Measuring the cares and joys of time.

"I go where God and glory shine;
His presence makes eternal day;
My all that's mortal I resign,
For angels wait and point my way."

LOUISA MUNDY.

[Born 1787. Died 1843. Came to India 1833. Laboured ten years.]

THE contrasts in life's early experiences among the chosen labourers in the vineyard of the Lord are beautiful and striking. Some, like Samuel, seem to receive the call in childhood, others in mature age, and now and then one comes on the stage at an advanced period in life's journey.

Louisa Kemp was among the latter, but her spiritual life was so deep, her course so beautifully consistent, and her active work so earnest and so blessed, that we must give her name a place among our best and choicest female missionaries.

She was not, like most of her sister-workers, descended from pious parents, or trained in an evangelical school; but she was, as a young woman, converted to God through a pious relative, and at once engaged in a course of earnest Christian labour, of a type that fitted her to enter on a wider sphere of fresh experiences in a heathen land.

The question was proposed to her, as a widow of forty-six, to become again a wife, and to go to India. It took her by surprise, but it was regarded as the answer to many prayers, in which she had besought the Lord to use her for His glory in any service He might appoint.

She was therefore ready to go forth, in 1833, as the wife of a missionary, to the sultry plains of Bengal, and she began her missionary course with bright and loving zeal. She studied diligently, and not unsuccessfully, the Bengali language; but her heavenly Father, who saw the burning love of her heart, pointed her to a sphere on which she could at once enter without it, and in this branch of service she spent the chief strength of her ten years of labour.

The blessing granted to her devoted work issued, in many instances, in striking cases of conversion among an unpromising class.

In the neighbourhood of Chinsurah, her husband's station, the first emigrants from Portugal had settled more than two centuries before. Among their descendants Mrs Mundy found the material for a much-needed school, and she conducted it herself under her own roof. This school gradually acquired celebrity, and though her pupils were nominally Roman Catholics, and extremely ignorant, prejudices were overcome by her unwearied efforts and her patient kindness.

In due time an infant school was added as a separate institution, and for years she could look upon eighty young immortals daily greeting her with their cheerful smiles.

Precious fruit was reaped from this interesting field, and many a bright spirit will have welcomed their loved teacher to the heavenly home they had attained through her guiding hand and heart.* But though these Christian schools, as they were called, were the chief employment of Mrs Mundy, she did not pass by the Hindus, and her native girls' school, where the little ones sat on mats under the thatched roof of an open building, was well attended, and did its part in overcoming prejudices, and preparing the way for entrance into the houses of Hindu gentlemen. At the present time the native ladies willing to be instructed in this locality are numerous.

Under the exhausting labours we have described, Mrs Mundy's strength gradually faded away, and in July 1843, after ten years of incessant toil, she sank without any decided disease, and gently breathed her redeemed spirit into the hands of that Saviour whom she so ardently loved and so faithfully served. There her eyes are satisfied with seeing, and her ears with hearing, the voice of that Mighty One who redeemed her to God through His blood.

And "I beheld, and lo, a great multitude, which no man could number, of all nations and kindreds, and people and tongues, stood before the throne, and before the Lamb, clothed with white robes, and palms in their hands; and cried with a loud voice, saying, Salvation to our God which sitteth upon the throne, and unto the Lamb."

* A Roman Catholic priest was also one of the fruits gathered from this school.

CHARLOTTE HÄBERLIN.

[Came to India 1839. Laboured sixteen years.]

CHARLOTTE KOELLNER was the daughter of one of those deeply, earnest, yet simple-minded Christian men with whom Württemberg abounds, and whose sons and daughters followed in his steps. She was the youngest, and was seen, even in childhood, to possess singular gifts and graces, which matured as she grew up.

She became the wife of Dr Häberlin, an Indian missionary, in 1838, and exercised a beautiful influence in this relationship. She obtained a good knowledge of, the native language, and translated Barth's "Scripture Stories" into excellent and idiomatic Bengali, thus enrolling herself among India's greatest benefactors by adding an invaluable book to its native Christian library.

A friend, who knew her intimately during the whole of her Indian career, thus writes:—

"My recollections of Mrs Häberlin's mental superiority, of her gentle kindness, and of her firm, unwavering friendship, are strong and ineffaceable. To her husband, often a decided invalid, and always in weak health, she was most helpful, entering into, and assisting him in, his varied efforts for the good of India. After his death, an event which took place under peculiarly painful circumstances, Mrs Häberlin undertook the office of Lady Superintendent of THE BETHUNE INSTITUTION in Calcutta, for native girls of good standing, and fulfilled her duties in this difficult position wisely and patiently. Her own family circle, if I may so call it, in Calcutta, consisted of native Christian and Eurasian or East Indian girls of various ages (one of the latter, a little foundling of about two years old), to whom she acted the part of a gentle and affectionate mother.

"In the Institution the direct teaching of Christianity was forbidden; but in the home circle the main object was to train the young people 'in the nurture and admonition of the Lord,' and to fit them in the various positions in which they might hereafter be placed, to become centres of Christian life and light.

"While thus engaged as superintendent, Mrs Häberlin's influence told in other directions, and young Hindu gentlemen solicited her help in giving Christian instruction to their wives in the evenings. This was to her a congenial, very encouraging, and hopeful labour, and was continued until she was suddenly summoned to Europe, on account of the death of her invaluable father, a touching memoir of whom was prepared by her own pen."

Her withdrawal from India rather quickened than deadened her interest in its people, and she dedicated and trained all her children for its service; but while thus delightfully employed, a son and a daughter, mere children, of ten and twelve years, but true and earnest Christians, were removed from her care to a higher; and a few years later her own health sank, and she followed them into the Saviour's presence.

Her eldest son, a gifted young man, was for several

years a missionary of the much-blessed German mission in Chota Nagpur, which was initiated by his father.

The peculiarly retiring disposition of Mrs Häberlin renders it nearly impossible to narrate much of her silent devotion to the missionary cause which was so dear to her heart.

A very intimate acquaintance with her in her daily life was necessary to adequately estimate her quiet zeal as a labourer in the Lord's vineyard; but there can be no doubt that she will meet ransomed ones from India's dark land, as her crown of rejoicing in that day when He shall count up His jewels.

HANNAH CATHERINE MULLENS.

[Born 1826. Died 1861. Aged 35.]

We now introduce to our readers a female missionary, in Calcutta, whose early life and surroundings stand in singular contrast to Mary Anne Wilson's or to Mary Bird's, yet one who was prepared by the Master she was to serve with no common service, and wonderfully adapted by Him for the part she was to take in raising India's daughters from their degradation.

Hannah Catherine Lacroix was born in Calcutta on the 1st of July 1826, when few advantages for training children existed in that city, so that her school education was imperfect, lasting but a single year. But she was the daughter of one of India's most gifted and devoted missionaries, and her early years were rich in the education of the heart, and in those wise and holy influences with which parents like hers, unconsciously as well as intentionally, encompass their children.

Amid the constant interruptions of domestic life, her gentle mother gave her the key to self-improvement, by teaching her to read, write, and use her needle, while she was daily gaining mental intelligence through the conversation of her father and his many friends. Yet her education, without a plan, led her in subsequent years to feel often at a loss in common things, such as the knowledge of localities, and of the dates of great events. Much as she regretted this, it proved no hindrance to her usefulness in the peculiar sphere she was destined to fill.

The powerful influence exercised by the vigorous, healthy character of her father, moulded and elevated her own. Her great intelligence caused her to acquire knowledge rapidly, and her smiling face and large bright eyes attracted towards her the notice and regard of her father's friends, most of whom were missionaries.

It often happened that a newly-arrived young man would engage the help of "little Hannah" in teaching him to pronounce the uncouth sounds of the vernacular, and her father made her his reader of any Bengali book he needed to be acquainted with, thus saving his own eyes, and increasing her readiness in the language.

As a child surrounded by Bengali servants, she

had learned to speak fluently, and when a day-school for girls was begun by her mother in their own garden, she asked permission to teach a class daily herself. Thus commenced, at the age of twelve years, that career of usefulness by which she afterwards became so greatly distinguished.

It was perhaps the missionary influences by which she was surrounded, and the loving nature which delighted to help others, that thus early called forth her youthful energies; but a year later a deeper motive touched her, and she learned to say, "The love of Christ constraineth me." A distinguished native preacher, Sujaat Ali, remembered in his prayer, at a meeting she attended, the children of missionaries, and pleaded earnestly for them.

That hour witnessed the yielding of her heart and all her powers to the Saviour and His work. Great natural modesty prevented her from at once alluding to this decision to others, but in her fifteenth year she united herself publicly to the service of her father's God.

In 1841 she enjoyed the privilege of visiting Europe; the influences on the voyage from missionary fellow-travellers helped to draw out her mental powers, and her stay in England, under judicious teachers, greatly enlarged her mind as well as her knowledge.

Her religious character, too, grew rapidly in spirituality and strength. A trip to Switzerland, in company with her parents, stirred her whole soul to its depths. The sight of the Bernese Alps, the first mountains she had ever seen, inspired her. Her impressions were embodied in a little journal, written in a peculiarly graphic and spirited manner, exhibiting the power which enabled her in more mature life to give those word-pictures of missionary scenes which have awakened the interest of so many youthful hearts.

On her return to Calcutta, being unable at once to open a girls' school, she formed a class of the female servants of the family and their children, and her Sundays were devoted to another class. In each case she succeeded in arousing in her scholars some of the earnestness which moved herself. Several of them died early, leaving her the joy of knowing that, in more than one or two instances, they had gone to the Saviour she had led them to trust for salvation.

Her union in 1845, in her nineteenth year, with Mr Mullens produced an extraordinary effect on her character and history. As a maiden, her great modesty had kept in check and even obscured the latent power she possessed. Her father's great superiority, and her intense respect and reverential love, had overshadowed the retiring spirit of the daughter; but in the companionship of the husband the quiet reserve disappeared. They read together, conversed together on the special work of each, and a new world seemed to open to her in history, science, and politics. She was also in an independent sphere, and labour and responsibility pressed upon her, calling out vigour of thought and imagination, deep religious feeling, and lofty, high-toned consecration.

All these rapidly developed. Her earnestness became enthusiasm; her affections, always strong, were exercised upon a wider range of objects, and she soon became known, not only as a good missionary's wife, but as a clever, lovable, and attractive woman.

In her girls' school she took the deepest interest, and there she laboured with diligence and delight. Her knowledge of Bengali made her quite at home among the girls, and this she increased by the careful study of its written literature. So correct and extensive did her acquaintance with it become, that her father often acknowledged, that if he could preach better than she could, her knowledge of words and idioms used in familiar conversation, of terms and expressions common among the story-loving and often angry women of the Hindu community, was much superior to his own.

Her school for the daughters of the native Christians soon became very popular. The number of her scholars rapidly increased from fourteen to twenty; thence to thirty, forty, and even more. She formed a Bible-class among the women of the Christian village, and endeavoured to instruct them regularly.

She kept steadily in view the position and sphere of life in which her scholars moved, and determined not to raise them above it, but elevate and improve them in it. She preserved, therefore, their native habits, introducing only such improvements as tended to make them more befitting the purity and comfort of Christian life. They wore the native dress, with the addition of a tight inner jacket; they sat on mats during their lessons; they slept on a dry boarded floor; were fed in native fashion; and all by turns shared in the duty of sweeping their rooms and cooking their food.

In instructing them, and that entirely in their own tongue, she sought to give the elements of general knowledge of Bible facts and Bible doctrine, and in manners to substitute a true modesty and reserve for that counterfeit which is only too common among Hindu women. This system was highly valued by the parents and friends of her scholars; it helped to increase their number, and its result was by degrees to introduce among the native churches of the mission many well-taught women who were the steady supporters of all efforts to raise the community at large. When well established, she was able, with the advance of public opinion among the converts, to add to it a little English, and some knowledge of fancy-work.

In one respect, she found her school not a hindrance, but a help. As her own children began to require companionship, she sought it among her girls, and was thus able not only to keep them free from harm, but in confidence and without anxiety to continue her labours in the school. The little service required of the girls was highly prized by them, because it furnished so many opportunities of intercourse with herself, and of gaining from her conversation the information on a thousand things which she was so ready to impart, and which was not called up by the ordinary routine of life in school.

Thus fitted, both by knowledge and experience, Mrs Mullens prepared her first Bengali work, "Phulmani and Karuna; a Book for Native Christian Women." In this little volume she desired to present to her readers a picture of a Christian and an un-Christian Hindu family, to display and argue against various forms of evil existing in the native communities, and so commend to them the excellence of Christian principle in the holy lives and happy deaths of its sincere disciples. This plan was carried out in the form of a story, most simply but most graphically told.

"In reading this little work," says a friendly critic, "we are transported at once to the heart of a Bengali Christian village. Bengali women and children walk lifelike in flesh and blood before us. The children run about, the women gossip, wrangle, and lie, or are honest, truthful, and industrious; but they are neither too bad nor too good for Bengali female nature as modified by Christianity.

"We are initiated into the mysteries of Bengali housekeeping, and begin to have becoming ideas of the value of a single farthing. We stand beside the deathbed of the righteous, and witness the woful end of the wicked, cut off unprepared in the midst of his sins.

"Christ, too, has a people in that little village; and the decency, industry, and good sense—the humble, active, cheerful piety which their lives show to be attainable and practicable in the poorest families, and under the most discouraging circumstances, can scarcely fail of leaving their moral in the most impervious mind.

"The leaven of heathenism, that still lingers in the nominal Christian, is delicately but clearly pointed out. Native customs and native prejudices, when injurious, are traced to their social and physical results with a happy simplicity. The story has all the lifelike minuteness and accuracy of Defoe; and the reader, if he has any spiritual relish, will find himself throughout in communication with a gentler and holier spirit than is commonly to be met with in our present imperfect state."

High as is the praise here given, it was not too high. The simple, beautiful, and idiomatic Bengali attracted the attention of the native converts immediately. Everywhere they were anxious to secure copies, and a large edition was put into circulation in a very short time.

Missionaries were delighted to obtain a book so completely adapted to the wants and position of their people, and made use of it even among the heathen. It was sought by labourers in other provinces of India; and by the multiplication of copies of the English MS., and by translation from one native tongue into another, it had, at the time of Mrs Mullens's death, been transferred into no less than twelve Indian languages, and was in full circulation among all the communities of converts throughout the land. Long will she speak to the Indian churches by this little volume, and long will the echoes of her footsteps sound among them now that her voice is hushed in death.

In 1852 Mrs Mullens's impaired health led her to accompany her children to England, and to visit her younger sisters, left there for education.

Her letters, so unaffected, so clear, so vivid, and her work, all had been to them a source of never-failing interest during their separation, and they were at home with her at once. "We were never weary," writes one of them, "of her long descriptions of the Indian home to which we were looking forward; and her freshness of thought, her bright imagination, and her Indian unconventionality, made her appear to us the most fascinating person we had ever seen.

"Her face was most attractive to us, from its ever-varying expression; her eyes, now soft and full of affection, then beaming with mirth; now animated and full of spirit, then wearing a strange, dreamy look, that showed her thoughts were far away, and that her active fancy was roaming amid other scenes. After a few months' delightful intercourse with old friends, and with her husband's family, whom she now learned to know for the first time, she parted from her two girls, and sailed for Calcutta, taking us and her little Eliot with her, at the beginning of 1854."

Again in India, she resumed her labours in the girls' school, and among the Christian women of the congregation, interrupted once alarmingly by an Indian fever, but blessed exceedingly in some touching instances of individual conversions, as well as in general results.

The same large number, increased at times to sixty Christian girls, resided with her; she saw them married, was gratified to find numbers of them doing well, some of them adorning the Gospel as consistent Christians; and as time advanced, she began to receive the children of her scholars of former days.

She warmly welcomed the converts coming forth from Hinduism, and endeavoured to do her part in softening to them the hard trial of quitting their families and homes for the Gospel's sake; she watched with thankful interest the growth of the little Christian village; and, as a true pastor's wife, visited its homes and families, that by kind counsel she might assist and guide them. She did not forget Bengali literature, and added to its Christian libraries two excellent works; one an original, both in English and Bengali, called, "The Missionary on the Ganges; or, What is Christianity?" the other a translation of "Daybreak in Britain," adapted from the English.

And yet, while thus able and willing to serve in the higher branches, she could write, "Nothing should be beneath us, done in our Master's service. In a worldly sense, one might have done something better than teach A B C all one's life; but in Christ's service, looking at it in the light of eternity, it becomes something noble, great, and grand. I could never have got on in life without the romance of religion to tinge all my work, and help me."

Mrs Mullens's narratives are graphic in the extreme, full of detail effectively arranged, and told in the most genial and hearty way. The feeling expressed is fervent and deep, the principle earnest, the tone of piety very elevated.

Her spirituality of mind appears very strongly in many of her letters; and very prominent also is that continued longing "to depart and be with Christ," which she cherished in her inmost soul for many years, and which she cared not to hide from the dear friends whom she loved as her own self.

To one such she wrote—

"How much we need a being to worship who shall be to us a warm, loving, understanding friend, and yet God too. A human heart is not strong enough for the burden we would impose, and in Him we find it! in THE MAN CHRIST JESUS! A GOD-MAN is exactly what I must have to supply my present need. I should like very much to go and see you; but if God willed, I would rather go to that better country where partings are unknown, and there await your coming. How soon the hours would pass, but here they seem so weary! Sin in our hearts is a dreadful enemy; sometimes it weighs more heavily than at others, and so I have felt it lately. I want to enjoy that sweetest of promises—We shall 'stand without fault before the throne of God.' But perhaps it is better to wait His pleasure than to seem impatient. I only desire to be prepared for the Bridegroom's coming—to have my lamp trimmed—to be found not slumbering, but watching." Most strikingly was her desire gratified.

In 1858 she again visited England, her husband being suddenly called home. Together they visited numerous places, and she was able, by her own enthusiasm, to give fresh stimulus to the interest already felt in her work. She visited mothers' meetings in London, and broke to them the bread of life; and as she spoke of Christ as the Saviour of the poor, the streaming eyes told that her words had penetrated their hearts.

To rich and poor alike she gave missionary addresses, forgetting she was a stranger, and gained in every case breathless attention, for she possessed in an eminent degree the power of fascinating her audience. She employed her quiet hours in preparing for a magazine "Missionary Pictures; or, Word-Paintings of Scenes in India, for the Young." "Oh how I love missionary-work!" she exclaims. "Missions are a passion with me, and I bless God that I have learned to labour on contentedly, without much visible success. It is the command, and not the results, with which we have to do, and I shall return joyfully to my Bengali women, if but to sow the merest germs of truth."

In 1861 she re-entered on her Indian work, recommenced her boarding-school with sixty girls, and found to her joy an unexpected opening into the new sphere she had longed for—the instruction of Hindu ladies in their own households. Before her visit to England she had for some time maintained two schools of respectable girls in private houses, and a few families in Calcutta had been visited for instruction by the members of the "Free Church Mission" and the "Calcutta Normal School."

On her return, she was delighted to find a great advance in Hindu public opinion respecting female education. A missionary's wife just leaving for England made over to her two families of Hindu ladies she had been accustomed to visit, and she soon gained access to several others in her own neighbourhood; indeed, zenana teaching, as it is termed, increased upon her hands so rapidly, that she accepted the help of a friend to share her duties in the boarding-school, and gave herself almost exclusively to this new and important sphere.

Some of the most interesting details of her daily visits to Hindu ladies are just alluded to in the history; but the time has not yet come for many particulars of this branch of missionary-work to be made public.*

Mrs Mullens had now reached the summit of her wishes, had become the intimate and trusted friend of many a secluded Hindu wife, and a welcome visitor into the most carefully-guarded apartments of Hindu gentlemen. The death of her honoured father, and of a beloved child, had chastened her already sanctified character to a still higher degree

* Mrs Mullens's labours, and its attendant success during this one year, would form a volume of thrilling interest. One striking incident which may be printed is added at the close of this memoir. It will illustrate what has been noticed of her graphic power.

of adaptation for her employment; and to the eye of her fellow-labourers she was the one to enter in and cultivate the new field with all its peculiarities, and to reap from it a rich and abundant harvest.

The brief period of her engagement in it sped rapidly away, marked by incidents of a most cheering character, and all was fair and bright before her, when He, whose thoughts are not as our thoughts, caused His voice to be heard by her, to come up higher, and to enter on a place and a work He had prepared for her in His own presence. The honour and the privilege she had so longed for, to be with Him, was awarded her. After some hours of suffering, from an illness which suddenly seized her while she was occupied in preparing a new book for the native women, to be finished by the end of the year, she was called to go in and see the King, to behold His glory, and to receive the reward of the good and faithful servant.

Thus, with very little delay, she laid down her mortal body and her charge together, and ceased at once to work and live. Need we say how she was mourned on earth, or try to describe the welcome that awaited her in heaven?

"The flower of Christ's flock in Bengal," "The most laborious and useful is gone," were the exclamations on all sides; but the Master had made no mistake, and the heavenly hosts worshipped Him in adoring gratitude and love, as they rejoiced in a new addition to the ranks of His redeemed, and heard a new voice uniting in the song, "To Him that loved us, and washed us from our sins in His own blood, and hath made us kings and priests unto God and His Father; to Him be glory and dominion for ever and ever. Amen."

Among the multitude who followed Mrs Mullens's remains to the grave were a hundred and fifty Hindu converts with their families, and the sermon, speaking of her bright example to survivors, was preached by a Hindu minister.

> "By the bright waters now thy lot is cast;
> Joy to thee, happy friend! thy bark hath past
> The rough sea's foam.
> Now the long yearning of thy soul is stilled;
> Home! home! thy peace is won, thy heart is filled;
> Thou art gone home!"

FIRST-FRUITS.

"While sitting at breakfast one morning in June, a singular letter was put into my hands. It ran thus: 'Madam,—I have taken the liberty of introducing the bearer of this. She is a Brahman widow, and belongs to a most respectable and wealthy family.

"'She has visited all the chief shrines of Hinduism, seeking rest for her soul, and finding none. She now turns to Christianity. Madam, will you receive her into your asylum? Will you teach her what truth is? I will just add one word for your own encouragement. There are other widows besides this one—ay, and there are married women too—

who are dissatisfied with, and restless in, their own religion. *They want something better.*—Yours, A Truth-Lover and a Truth-Seeker.'

"'Ask the bearer to come in,' said I, hardly knowing what to expect.

"A gentle-looking, modest woman entered the room. She seemed about twenty-four, and her every word and action showed the Hindu *lady*, though she looked hot, wearied, and very much excited.

"'Was the letter I brought addressed to *you?* she inquired. 'Yes.' 'Then I will wait till you have finished breakfast, for I must see you alone. I can easily wait.'

"To try her, I said, 'You must go away to-day, and come again to-morrow. I have an unavoidable engagement. I am sorry, but I have not even five minutes to speak to you now.'

"'Then I will wait—wait as long as you like. I have been waiting for this all my life. It would be hard to wish me to go away when I have found what I sought.'

"I left her. Hopes, doubts, fears rose in my heart, and but one prayer came to my lips, again and again, and yet again—'Holy Spirit, is not Thy promise pledged? Oh, breathe upon this soul; then shall it live and blossom and bear fruit.' My engagement was to hear a catechist's trial sermon to the heathen servants of an English lady. His text was, 'Yet the dogs eat of the crumbs which fall from their master's table;' and as I heard, I thought of the waiting one at home, and it seemed to me as if the answer to my prayer had already come, and that Jesus was saying to that one, 'O woman, great is thy faith; be it unto thee even as thou wilt.'

"I was soon back. It took three hours to hear the Brahmanee's strange sad story, with all its thrilling interest. Hers had been eminently a life of *seeking.* Had she found at last the hidden treasure? Left a widow at fourteen years of age, her penances, and her austerities had commenced, though otherwise she was kindly treated; but ever since she had thought at all, she had been dissatisfied with Hinduism. And when the death of her husband left her free, and comparatively wealthy, she had begun to visit the various holy places celebrated in Hindu story, with a view to find out whether they could give her that soul-rest which was denied to her at home.

"Her account of this search after spiritual peace was often most touching. Once, she said, when she was a little girl, her elder sister was dangerously ill, and her parents took her to a distant shrine to join her prayers with theirs for the recovery of their child. The idol was propitious; the sister got well, and Bossonto believed in that idol. In after years, when God sent this longing for truth into her heart, she bethought herself of the being who had once, as she considered, heard her prayer, and she again repaired to his shrine.

"They told her his most acceptable worshippers were those who approached him fasting. For two whole days she fasted, and this time her prayer was, 'Teach me thy way, O God.' On the third day she fainted, with that prayer for light and guidance still on her lips. 'Now,' she asked, 'may not the unknown God, to whom I then prayed, have heard my prayer, and brought me here in answer to it?' I was silent. How could I tell? Though this I knew, that 'God looketh on the heart.'

"Not wishing to trust my own judgment merely, I asked two of the native preachers, who had been themselves Brahmans, to be present at this conversation. They saw nothing in her story improbable, or unworthy of belief; and, by a strange coincidence, it was found that Bossonto was distantly related to one of them. He knew her family, and could vouch for its respectability and wealth. Bossonto was then asked about the writer of that strange letter. She was afraid it would bring him into trouble with his own people, therefore it was with considerable reluctance she gave his name, and that only when she was assured that it was absolutely necessary.

"He proved to be a Brahman, well known to the mission family. We were aware that he knew the truth, but not that he had felt its power, or that he had any love for it. Surprised, therefore, were we to hear that it was from this man's wife that Bossonto had first learned Christianity. Her husband had taught her; and when her widowed friend had told her of her doubts respecting Hinduism, and her longings for a religion that would satisfy the wants of her soul, she said, 'Bossonto, Christianity is the religion for you. Go and be a Christian. I only wish we could be Christians too; but alas! we have too many ties of caste and family. You are free, do go,' and then the husband gave her that letter of introduction. She had got away from home by implying that she was going on a pilgrimage to Banares. That was a holy purpose. They were used to her ways, and let her go.

"Such was Bossonto's account of herself. The next step was to try and discover whether it was all true. One of the native preachers kindly undertook this, and rode many miles for the purpose. The result was perfectly satisfactory. At that time Bossonto's state of mind was that of a humble learner. It was not that she knew much of Christianity, but it was as if what her heathen friend had told her had also been revealed to her by a far higher power, that Jesus was the only Saviour for her sin-sick soul, and she sought after the Lord, if haply she might feel after Him and find Him.

"After three months' residence in our family, every day increases our love and affection for her. Naturally very clever and intelligent, she has learned to read her Bible in an incredibly short time; it is rarely out of her hands, and each morning may find her taking her place among the girls of the native Christian boarding-school, to get the benefit of their daily Bible lessons.

"Every now and then she looks up, with extreme earnestness depicted on her bright face, to ask, 'Oh, do you think this blind one will ever see? Do you think I shall ever understand it at all?' She may know it not, but the Spirit has already taught her to behold wondrous things out of His law; for she said on one occasion, 'I think I see the difference between the Hindu Shastras and the Book of God. Is it not this—the former is filled with outward ceremonies, which cannot make the heart better; while the latter has to do *chiefly* with the heart—how it can be purified and made fit to dwell with God?'

"When asked what made her first think that idols were not true gods, she replied, 'Because I saw the glorious sun, moon, and stars. Not only so, but I saw that all these were governed by certain *laws;* the planets went round the sun, and the tides were influenced by the moon; then I knew that there must be one Being greater in the universe than any I had yet heard of.'

"But this was not the feeling that had brought her to the feet of Jesus. To Him she came on account of her *need*, her *want;* and Christians will understand her, though she often says, 'I wish I could express myself better, but I do not know what else to say, than that I have been *needing* the true religion all my life, and now I have found it.'"

LOUISA GOMEZ.

[Born 1836. Died 1873. Aged 37.]

We have as yet only mentioned among our eminent female missionaries those from Europe or America, who were moved by sympathy and allured by love to cross the sea out of compassion to their heathen sisters. We now rejoice to place on record the name of one who never saw any country but India, and was familiar with its language and its people from her birth.

In the Memoir of Louisa Mundy we read of a class descended from Portuguese settlers of an early date, on whose teaching she spent her strength—to this class belonged Louisa Gomez.

Varied, both by nation and character, are the chosen vessels our Lord uses to work in His vineyard, for there is no respect of persons with Him, and that He delights to honour one as well as another is manifest by the blessing He gave to the faithful service of Louisa Gomez. She was born in Calcutta about the year 1836, of Indo-Portuguese parents, who were strict Roman Catholics; but was allowed to attend a school formed by a Protestant clergyman, the Rev. R. B. Boswell, in the hope of conveying spiritual light and life to the numerous persons of this class living near his church.

A devoted Christian mistress, who shared his feeling, laboured in this school for many years, and to her teaching and holy influence we trace the spiritual blessing which gradually distilled on Louisa's heart. A touchy and perverse temper had to be overcome, and the mists of a deeply-prejudiced mind had to be cleared by the patient, loving teacher, who, after years of effort, rejoiced to observe the penitential tear, and to note the rising desire for pardon and for peace.

The 18th chapter of Revelation had arrested the

girl's attention, and so impressed her mind, that she refused to attend the Roman Catholic church, and was led to pray for "a little light" and "a believing heart." Her prayer was heard; she gave herself to the Lord, and besought Him, if it pleased Him, to make her a new, sharp, threshing instrument in His hand, and to engage her in bringing others to Him. Thus decided in her Christian character, she was chosen as a monitress, and finally, at the age of nineteen, was recommended to the Normal School in Calcutta, to be trained as a future worker among native women.

Louisa's docile, grateful disposition, and patient, persevering habits, commended her to the love of the Normal School teachers, who valued her example and influence greatly. Her natural infirmity of temper was not quite overcome, but it was mourned over and repented of before God, who strengthened her for conflict, and finally gave the victory. Her thirst for knowledge, and diligent study of God's Word and of the Bengali language, enabled her after three years' training to attain the longed-for success, and after passing her examinations and gaining her certificate in English and Bengali, she became the regular teacher of the Bengali Christian Girls' School.

Here she acquired greater facility in the language, and an "aptness to teach" which prepared her to enter upon the higher branch of zenana visitation, when the houses of native gentlemen so rapidly opened as to require the whole time and energy of those, fitted as she was, to carry on efficiently this branch of work. She had laboured with self-devotion and success in her school, and in her daily instruction of several families of high-caste ladies she displayed such an amount of tact, zeal, and love, as rendered her a valuable and much-prized worker. The toil of years in training was abundantly repaid in her case by witnessing the delight with which her pupils heard and read the story of redeeming love.

Louisa loved better to work than to write, and the nature of that work does not permit publicity to interesting details of individual cases in which she had the joy of leading precious souls to the Saviour. She witnessed the conversion of many, some of whom confessed Christ openly by baptism, in spite of much opposition and persecution.

Of her it may be truly said that she was "in labours more abundant," and she had also that happy faculty of a good worker, of cutting out fresh work and finding new paths for her abundant energy.

Thus, in 1868, she says, after giving an account of the distribution of her time—"Every Saturday I have a Bible-class for Christian women in the village near the Normal School, and about twelve or fourteen come, many of whom are very attentive, and seem to have an interest in Bible truths. May God in His good time bring these poor women into the fold of the good Shepherd.

"The Bible-class for teachers I have only on Mondays. There is so much to be done in the way of spreading the Gospel of our blessed Lord and Saviour, that, had I ten thousand lives, I would devote them all gladly to His service. I am very thankful to you for promising to assist me with your prayers while I am engaged in teaching our poor heathen sisters the way of salvation through our dear Lord and Saviour Jesus Christ. My fellow-labourers and I need this help, that God might cause His mighty Spirit to come down like showers upon the inhabitants of India, that souls might be converted and brought into the fold of Christ."

In 1869 she writes—"You will be glad to learn that the mission-work in India is increasing very rapidly. . . . . To-day it is just a fortnight since I opened a school at Echhapur, and it now consists of forty-two children from the ages of five to twelve. They are all high-class children, who value education more than the lower. To-day they looked so bright and happy when I was giving them a scripture lesson. I have also three zenanas open, and though I can only go on Saturdays, a Christian teacher lives there, and carries on the work during my absence."

In 1869 Miss Gomez opened a Hindu school not very far from the "Home." She went at seven o'clock in the morning, and stayed till nine, teaching forty girls.

And all this was in addition to her regular work of zenana visitation, in which she spent the whole day.

Again, in 1869, she writes to the same friend—"It is sweet to go on working, knowing that our work will not be in vain in the Lord, though there are many disappointments. Two of my other zenanas, in which the ladies took a deep interest in the Bible, are closed. The parents were afraid when they found their daughters were drawn towards Christianity, and stopped their lessons; both of the pupils expressed great grief in not being able to learn the way of God more perfectly, but they promised to read the New Testament, which I left with them at their desire. In the midst of these discouragements I have this comfort: I have left my Saviour and His Word with them, and if they are His, they will never be lost.

"I am thankful to be able to add that two more of my zenana ladies have been lately admitted into the visible Church of Christ by baptism. Their husbands had been baptized a year ago, and now they and their wives are walking in the fear of the Lord: their little ones were baptized with the mothers.

"I have also three houses where they do love to hear of Jesus; and two or three of the ladies, I believe, love the Saviour, and pray to Him. One of them, I do not doubt, is a true follower of Jesus, though she has not yet the courage to come out and be baptized. Pray do not cease to plead for all these dear ones, especially the last. The work at Echhapur is getting on nicely, though at times, being weak in faith, my heart sinks under its difficulties; but God is good and faithful; He does not leave me long, but sends fresh comfort and encouragement from unexpected quarters, and I am not worthy of the least of all His mercies. Pray for me."

Extracts of the same character from Miss Gomez's letters and reports might be greatly multiplied, but these are sufficient to show the prayerful, loving spirit in which she carried on the work, and how true and faithful she was to the one great object of bringing precious souls to Christ. Nothing short of this ever seemed to satisfy her. And God gave her the desire of her heart in a remarkable degree, so that I believe we may truly say no zenana missionary has ever been more successful in leading souls to Christ.

And thus, carried on by herself and her devoted coadjutors, the work grew and prospered abundantly, extending to the suburbs of Calcutta as far as Agurparah, Sodepur, and Barrackpur to the north, Howrah to the west, Thakurpukar to the south; so that, whereas in 1861 there were eight zenanas under instruction, with an average of five pupils in each, in 1865 the report says—

"We visited thirty-three zenanas, and were privileged to teach one hundred and one of their inmates; and in 1869 the number of zenanas open in Calcutta was a hundred, with three hundred and thirty pupils!"*

When the work at Barrackpur was first commenced, Miss Gomez and her assistants used to visit it from Calcutta once or twice a week, and a native Christian woman was placed there to take charge of, and give instruction to, the school.

But the work increased so rapidly, that it was found desirable there should be a resident teacher on the spot. Accordingly a house was taken, and Miss Gomez went to live there with two or three native

* This simply refers to the one society with which she was connected; others at work had equal encouragement.

assistants. At the close of 1870 Mrs Sandys writes—"I do not know if you are aware how great an institution Barrackpur has become. Miss Gomez has, besides Miss Francis, eight native teachers living in the house, and employs two gharries, three horses, &c."

Of the work itself Miss Gomez says—"I have Miss Francis and my native teachers to help me, and I believe our work will prosper in God's own good time. We meet with a great many discouragements, but thanks to 'Him who is faithful,' and who has promised success to those who look to Him for guidance. Jeremiah i. 17-19 has been a great support to us in the midst of trial, especially the last verse. We have here at present forty houses and three schools."

In 1871 the work at Barrackpur had almost doubled! There were eighty houses and five schools under instruction; and Miss Gomez was assisted by her two nieces, Miss Morris and Miss Adams, the expense of whose training at the Normal School she herself had borne.

And here we may notice one beautiful and uncommon feature of her character, viz., her generosity and freedom from mercenary feeling. This led her to decline an increase of salary when it was offered to her. As she said, "she had enough for all her wants." She dedicated the tenth of her income to the service of God, and she tried to induce others to do the same, saying, when urging it upon her niece, "You know I always have enough, and any time you are in want, you may call on me for help."

Of the work at Barrackpur, she writes in 1871—"The Lord has indeed owned the feeble efforts of

His unworthy servants, and is still showering down His rich blessing upon us in this station, both temporally and spiritually, 'for a great door and effectual is opened unto us, and there are many adversaries.'" She then proceeds to give further particulars, and says—"Some of my zenana ladies here are very intelligent, and pay great attention to their Scripture lessons; in three or four of them, I believe, I can see the working of the Spirit of God."

The report of 1873 has a peculiar and touching interest from being the last ever penned by this faithful and devoted servant of the Lord. She begins it by saying—

"I must ask all friends to join in praising God for the help He has given during the year that has just closed.

"In the midst of great difficulties and much casting down, He has given us fresh proofs of His faithfulness and love, and has permitted me to see that some of my pupils are growing in grace and in the knowledge of our Lord and Saviour Jesus Christ, whilst some new ones have been added to their number.

"We closed the year with ninety-six houses, with two hundred and thirty-six pupils, and four schools, with about seventy children. The numbers of both zenana and school pupils would have been more if there had not been so much sickness among them; the people are still suffering from fever."

Many interesting particulars of individual cases of conversion, following upon her prayerful and patient efforts, and those of her fellow-workers, are then given, and she concludes her report with this remarkable sentence—

"Barrackpur work is very encouraging, notwithstanding the constant opposition we meet with. 'The battle is the Lord's,' and He will fight for us."

It is affecting to think how soon this valiant soldier of the cross was to lay down her arms. In 1872 she had a severe attack of dengue fever, but she writes—"The Lord dealt very lovingly with me during my illness, and He has restored my strength to do His work." She seems, however, never to have recovered from this attack.

On returning to Calcutta she resumed her beloved work, but complained of constant headache, and was so depressed in spirits that she could not eat or sleep. At length mind and body were so evidently overwrought that her medical adviser prescribed absolute rest and change of scene.

The sequel is touchingly told in a letter from one of the native Christian converts, who regarded her as a mother in Christ, and who had been her assistant at Barrackpur. It is a translation—

"My very kind Friend,—I have tidings to give you that will dry up all joy; it is that my loved teacher, being weak and ill, went to recruit at Banares, and afterwards proceeded to Roy Bareilly. She had to cross a river, and it being a dark night, she remained in the boat, telling the boatman to anchor and go to rest, as she would do.

"All went to sleep, and how it happened that our beloved 'Mem' fell into the river and was drowned, no one can tell. In the morning they sought her in vain—she was gone; only her things were there. The boatman carried the news to Roy Bareilly, and Mr Plomer went and searched the river for two days, but no trace was to be seen.

"We know that she is safe with the Lord—but oh! what grief that I was not with her at the time of her death! When she was leaving us to go to Banares, she put her hands on my head and Bindu's, and blessing us, said, 'The Lord be with you; place all your burden on Him, and keep near Him; I have given you into His hands.' So saying, she left us.

"You know all she was to me, far more than words of mine can tell. Her loss causes me now to float on the sea of sorrow. When a mother dies, the child cannot but drink the cup of woe, and my cup is very full. She was my guide; when I became careless, and mixed with the world, she recalled and roused me, but I know the Lord is my salvation, and will ever keep me.

"As the lotus cannot support itself without the stem, so the Lord put us into her care; she was our stem. The Lord has seen meet to break our stay. Our comfort is that in a little while in heaven we shall be reunited."

A letter from Mrs Sandys, who had for years been her kind and sympathising friend and adviser, and who had ample opportunities, by personal acquaintance, for thorough knowledge of Miss Gomez and her work, will conclude our notice of this interesting woman :—

"I think through my whole life the thought of dear Miss Gomez as the most earnest missionary I have ever seen will continue. Literally her meat and drink was to do the work of God.

"She often came to us to stay a day or two (sometimes only for some hours) to recruit, when quite exhausted by her labours; and at such times her best restorative seemed to be if I could tell her of any more openings, either for her or myself to make Christ known to our poor heathen friends. Immediately fatigue was forgotten in her eagerness to be up and doing.

"She had no great talents or remarkable gifts; but she had that rare qualification of singleness of aim and oneness of purpose which ever gives force and dignity to a life, and resulted in that entire consecration of herself, body and soul, to the service of her dear Lord and Master, which could not fail to produce lasting results.

"I know she prayed much for each and all of her pupils, which no doubt was the reason of her success in leading them to Jesus. Their trials and difficulties she entered into most feelingly. I used to think her own early experience of persecution by relatives made her peculiarly alive to these; they touched her to the quick.

"She was wont to come and tell us all the sad circumstances of a case, and then entreat us to PRAY for the dear one, and realised so fully that the Lord would make a way of escape, and that in His time the heathen sister would be permitted to acknowledge her belief in Christ. I think she had much wisdom in directing such, neither urging a too hasty avowal, nor, on the other hand, encouraging anything like shrinking from bearing the reproach of the cross."

> "Servant of God, well done,
> Rest from thy loved employ!
> The battle fought, the victory won,
> Enter thy Master's joy!"

ALICE MARY WADE.

[Born 1850. Died 1871. 1870–71.]

"I AM come that they might have life, and that they might have it more abundantly" (literally, "in full abundance"). Surely this precious utterance of the Lord Jesus Christ found its fulfilment in dear Alice Mary Moore, His loving missionary at home, then to the perishing women in India, and now serving Him in a higher, brighter sphere among the ransomed ones in heaven.

It is beautiful to observe how the Master seems to have set her specially apart for His service from her earliest days, giving her the blessing of believing, earnest-hearted parents, who devoted all their energies to the Christian training of their children. Even in childhood she loved holy things, and as she grew in years grew steadily and continuously in grace; so that when but fifteen it was remarked of her that all she undertook was in the spirit of "this one thing I do," and it was easy to see that her longing desire was to lead sinners to the feet of Jesus. The true missionary spirit, manifested in unwearied activity and zeal, was, even at this early age, ever burning within her; while the marked spirituality of her character, and the simplicity of her Christ-like behaviour, was also strikingly apparent.

Her ready help was soon claimed by all around her for school-work, district visiting, &c., and her bright and joyous spirit gave a charm to her loving efforts in the Sunday day and night schools. The people and their children were attracted by her winning, sympathising ways; and a still richer reward was given her, in seeing many of them won to Christ Himself, the Light she always carried with her in her ministrations. She learned of the Master that she might be able to teach His grace to others; Bible-classes and Christian meetings were a delight to her. Many MS. books did she fill with copious notes of all she learned through these opportunities.

But as home-mission work deepened in interest, a fresh chord of sympathy was touched in Alice's heart. She heard of the condition of her Hindu sisters, and longed to help rescue them from their degradation.

From that moment the welfare of the poor zenana inmates became to her an object of deep and prayerful interest, and in the autumn of 1870 she consented to become the helpmeet of an Indian missionary, the Rev. T. R. Wade, then in England for a while, but soon to return to his station in Peshawur. She rejoiced in the prospect of entering the missionary field, and shrank not from the pain of severing home ties, though loving, and beloved by her family in no common degree; she recognised the Master's call, and at His bidding she set forth, impelled by a love higher and deeper than the dear human love, even the constraining love of Christ.

In October 1870, Mr Wade and his young wife started for India. After a prosperous voyage, during which Alice made several "friendships for eternity," they reached Bombay, thence proceeding slowly through Nasik and its neighbouring Christian village, Sharanpur, Allahabad, Lucknow, Agra, Delhi, Umritsur, and Lahore, to their own station in the Punjaub.

At each place they had made some stay, and she had eagerly visited the various zenanas and schools, gaining information and experience. Her knowledge of Hindustani, which she began to study in England, enabled her to converse with the natives, though but imperfectly; but her interest in the zenana women, deep when at home, was intensified on finding herself in actual contact with these poor uncared-for sisters. Her letters home, and the ample details in her journal of her visits to them, testify to the love and sympathy they called out.

Arrived at her station, she entered at once on the visitation of the schools and native females, throwing herself with zeal and joyful alacrity into the work to which she had set her hand. As in

London, so in Peshawur, she gained the hearts of fellow-labourers, her own work being truly one of love. Her interesting account of her school was published in 1871, but our limits do not permit its introduction here. Her kindness of heart, making her ready to become all things to all men, if by any means she might gain some, was shown when her presence was one day sought to mourn with a native lady who had lost her son. She went to the house of sorrow, and joined with the family in spending what must have been to her a very depressing and irksome morning, feeling, as she touchingly wrote, that "Ourselves your servants for Christ's sake" was a good motto for missionaries.

She soon began a normal class in Peshawur, and obtained a native Christian teacher from Agra, showing in all her work a great talent for organisation, and an eminent fitness for the sphere in which the Lord had placed her, though conscious of the deadening influence of a crowd of heathen and careless ones on all sides, a danger to which happily she never succumbed.

From June to the end of September Mr and Mrs Wade were absent, to escape the excessive heat of Peshawur. The return journey was a trying one, but on the 7th October she enjoyed a Scripture reading greatly, and her conversation indicated the spiritual and happy tone of her mind. Referring to the death of her father, tidings of which, when first received, had caused her intense pain, she said, "I have almost ceased to grieve for dear papa, he has his heart's desire—he is with the Saviour he so longed to join," afterwards adding, "He does not seem very far away." A friend remarked—

> "I change, He changes not;
> The Christ can never die."

Her whole face lighted up, and with much depth of feeling she added—

> "His love, not mine, the resting-place;
> His truth, not mine, the tie."

The following morning, Sunday the 8th October, this kind friend read with her John xvii. At the twentieth verse, she said, "I am so fond of that verse," and then spoke of wishing to take the Lord's Supper. It was agreed that this should be the great object of their coming together.

She was not well, but able to enjoy conversation as she lay on the sofa; then in a moment convulsions seized her. Remedies were applied, and she sat up, whispering, "Pray;" but the ebbing life could not be stayed, and before many moments she quietly passed away. Thus early * went her loving spirit up to God who gave it—up to Him who loved her and had need of her—up to the Master for whom she had gladly spent herself and her life. What the loss was to the Church, to her husband, her widowed mother, and others, we may not say; but to all comes the comfort, "*Blessed* are the dead that die in the Lord." Her chief, her all-absorbing joy had been work for

* Her age was about twenty-one.

the Master, her sorrow that she could not serve Him without hindrance.

Now that the struggle of sin with her is over, now that she sees face to face the King in His beauty, now that she has the desire of her earnest loving heart, to serve Him without weariness, and praise Him without sin—who that has the same longing, though ever so feeble, who that owns the same Master, though loving Him ever so imperfectly, could wish that her reward had been delayed, and herself not yet perfected in Christ? May we all, at home or abroad, be imbued with her missionary spirit, and, by the grace of God, which was able to accomplish such bright things in her, be led to follow her as she followed Christ.

APPENDIX.

It was intended to give in an appendix some letters from native Christian lady-teachers in India to friends in England, but we substitute the following description, just received from a German missionary, of a

CHRISTMAS TREAT FOR ZENANA LADIES AT LUCKNOW.

"Mrs Dæuble gave her annual entertainment at the Zahúr Bakhsh, on the 30th of December, to the Begams and the zenana school-children in connection with the Church Missionary Society and the Indian Female Normal School and Instruction Society. The object of the entertainment, in addition to its being an expression of kindly feeling and mutual good-will, is to give the ladies of the zenana an opportunity of meeting English ladies outside their own homes, and enjoying a change of scene and occupation. The zenana ladies seemed to appreciate the opportunity, for they mustered to the number of fifty-eight, besides several of their friends and children; and as they all came in carriages and palkies, with a considerable number of servants carrying the all-important pawn-box with its various contents, while not a single male person was allowed to come near to keep order or preside over the process of unloading, the scene was not wanting in excitement and vivacity. Several of the Begums came as early as three o'clock, and were taken to the roof of the Zahúr Bakhsh, where they were delighted with a view which was more interesting to them than the everlasting square whitewashed courtyard, which is all that they are generally able to refresh their eyesight with. Coming down-stairs again, they found a spacious apartment filled with girls from the Church Mission Society Female Schools, and decorated with an immense tree covered with flags, balls, and presents in all shapes and colours, the walls ornamented with texts in Roman, Persian, and Hindi characters, wreaths of flowers and gay banners, tables loaded with fruit and sweetmeats, and a harmonium which was played by one of the ladies of the mission for the amusement of the visitors. The dresses of some of the Begums were extremely rich and gorgeous, with a profusion of gold, while a few had gold powder sprinkled over their faces. The proceedings were opened by the singing of a hymn in Hindustani by the school-children, but the serious business of the evening was (as perhaps it should have been) incessant and inexhaustible talk—talk with one another, and talk with the ladies who were present. It is, we believe, a common idea of male persons that the ladies of the zenana are soft, delicate, speechless, down-trodden, cowering, dovelike, caged creatures, without a spark of vivacity or interest in human affairs. If such people could have been present on this occasion—which they could not—they would have had to change their opinion, and to admit that zenana ladies have a remarkable capacity, perhaps even appetite, for at any rate that phase of public life which is seen in large entertainments. There were indeed here and there two or three quiet, retiring creatures, who got themselves talked into a headache; but the majority of the native ladies present displayed both great activity in creating loud conversation and great fortitude in enduring it. When the time comes for the ladies of India to come out into public life, which of course it must some day, the majority will be found much less unprepared for its difficulties and its duties than is now generally imagined. That is one very important lesson which these gatherings have taught the missionaries. Perhaps they are also entitled to believe, from their experience of these entertainments, that the destined emergence of purdah ladies into their proper sphere of action may be a very rapid one; at any rate, it is worth noting that two years ago only seven ladies could be induced to come, while now fifty-eight came without any difficulty at all.

"Presents of work-materials were distributed to the school-children, while the zenana ladies were gratified with fancy articles of various kinds. The entertainment lasted from five to eight P.M. The visitors, including a number of native Christian ladies, amounted to more than two hundred."

THE END.

April, 1875.

A SELECTION FROM

JAMES NISBET AND CO.'S CATALOGUE.

TWELVE MONTHS IN MADAGASCAR. By the Rev. Dr. MULLENS, Foreign Secretary of the London Missionary Society. Post 8vo, cloth, with Illustrations.

SERMONS. By the late Rev. GEORGE MAXWELL, Vicar of Winterborne, Whitchurch, Dorset. Edited by his DAUGHTER. Crown 8vo, 4s. 6d. cloth.

SHOWERS OF BLESSING. A Book for the Times. By the Rev. W. LANDELS, D.D. Crown 8vo, 1s. sewed; 1s. 6d. cloth.

MISSIONARY WORK IN THE ZENANA. By Mrs. WEITBRECHT. Crown 8vo, cloth.

THE SAINTLY CALLING. By the Rev. C. D. BELL, M.A., Rector of Cheltenham, and Hon. Canon of Carlisle. Crown 8vo, 3s. 6d. cloth.

THE GOLDEN CHAIN. By the Author of "Memorials of Captain Hedley Vicars," "Crossing the River," &c. Crown 8vo, 1s. 6d. cloth.

"The links of this chain are mainly composed of touching and instructive incidents."—*Christian.*

NURSES FOR THE NEEDY; or, the Bible Women Nurses in the Homes of the London Poor. By L. N. R., Author of "The Missing Link." Crown 8vo, 3s. 6d. cloth.

"Some of the sketches given are touching in their tenderness, while they are all instructive in a high degree."—*Edinburgh Daily Review.*

MORNING BELLS AND LITTLE PILLOWS;

being Waking and Good Night Thoughts for the Little Ones. By FRANCES R. HAVERGAL. Royal 32mo, each 6d. sewed; 9d. cloth.

"They are written in so affectionate and interesting a way that the youthful reader cannot fail to become more and more delighted as each successive page is perused."—*Christian Standard.*

CLEFTS OF THE ROCK; or, The Believer's Grounds

of Confidence in Christ. By the Rev. J. R. MACDUFF, D.D., Author of "The Gates of Prayer," etc. Crown 8vo, 5s. cloth.

"Is rich in illustration, and will form a welcome present to devout readers."—*Freeman.*

THE PIRATE CITY. An Algerine Tale. By R. M.

BALLANTYNE, Author of "Black Ivory," &c. With Illustrations. Crown 8vo, 5s. cloth.

"The tale is told with Mr. Ballantyne's usual facility."—*Athenæum.*
"The story is of thrilling interest."—*Graphic.*

THE RENT VEIL. By the Rev. H. BONAR, D.D.,

Author of "The Christ of God," &c. Crown 8vo, 3s. cloth.

"Simple and direct in its style, rich in its Biblical theology, and ripe in its spiritual experience."—*English Presbyterian Messenger.*

SEED-TIME IN KASHMIR; a Memoir of WILLIAM J.

ELMSLIE, M.D., F.R.C.S.E., etc., late Medical Missionary of the C. M. S. in Kashmir. By His WIDOW and Dr. W. BURNS THOMSON, Medical Missionary. Crown 8vo, 4s. 6d. cloth.

"A very interesting, stimulating, and profitable biography."—*Christian Treasury.*

HOLDEN WITH THE CORDS. By W. L. M. JAY,

Author of "Shiloh." Post 8vo, 7s. 6d. cloth.

"Is very vigorously written, full of thought and beauty, and enriched with a considerable variety of character."—*Guardian.*

THE CHRISTIAN LIFE. An Exposition of Bunyan's

"Pilgrim's Progress." By Rev. JAMES BLACK, D.D., Glasgow. Volume II. completing the work. Post 8vo, 7s. 6d. cloth.

EDDA. Tales of a Grandmother. A History of Denmark.

Edited by PHILOJUVENIS. New Edition, with Illustrations. 4to. 10s. 6d. cloth.

"A worthy book, with delightful illustrations, which carry the eye to many amusing anecdotes."—*Guardian.*

SCEPTRES AND CROWNS, AND THE FLAG OF TRUCE. By the Author of the "Wide Wide World." With Coloured Illustrations. Crown 8vo, 3s. 6d. cloth.

"The teaching is exceedingly skilfully conveyed, and evangelical in tone, ... delightfully written, and full of simple grace."—*Freeman.*

A MEMOIR OF THE RIGHT REV. ROBERT DALY, D.D., LATE LORD BISHOP OF CASHEL, etc. By Mrs. HAMILTON MADDEN, Author of "Personal Recollections of the Bishop of Cashel." Post 8vo, 7s. 6d. cloth.

"The author furnishes much that is interesting and valuable."—*Rock.*

BERTRAM, THE HEIR OF PENDYNE. A Tale. Crown 8vo, 5s. cloth.

"A very pleasing, well-written, and most interesting tale, ... the religious tone is good, reverent, and practical."—*Record.*

GOD'S WORK, AND HOW TO DO IT. A Tale illustrating the Happy Results of Confirmation. By the Rev. WILLIAM GRAY, M.A., Vicar of St. John's, Wembley. Crown 8vo, 3s. 6d. cloth.

"An excellent tale, ... a seasonable and interesting book, and one so well calculated to be useful at that very critical period of a girl's life, her preparation for confirmation."—*Record.*

REAL PICTURES OF CLERICAL LIFE IN IRELAND. By J. DUNCAN CRAIG. D.D., Author of "La Debonâdo." Crown 8vo, 7s. 6d. cloth.

"Thoroughly interesting, and full of instruction for those who care to learn."—*Rock.*

FOUR YEARS IN ASHANTEE. By the Missionaries RAMSEYER and KÜHNE. Post 8vo, cloth.

URBANÉ AND HIS FRIENDS. By Mrs. PRENTISS, Author of "Stepping Heavenward," &c. With Coloured Illustrations. Crown 8vo, 2s. 6d. cloth.

"The coloured pictures are very good, and the little volume would make a good present to a girl, showing as it does how a true influence tells in the end."—*Nonconformist.*

EARTH'S MORNING; or, Thoughts on Genesis. By the Rev. HORATIUS BONAR, D.D., Author of "Light and Truth," &c. Crown 8vo, 5s. cloth.

"The expositions of words and phrases are marked by much solid learning."—*Weekly Review.*

A SOLDIER'S EXPERIENCE OF GOD'S LOVE AND OF HIS FAITHFULNESS TO HIS WORD. By C. H. MALAN, once a Major in the British Army. Crown 8vo, 3s. 6d., cloth.

"It is full of incident, and pervaded by a fine religious spirit."—*Daily Review.*

HILLS THAT BRING PEACE. By the Rev. CHARLES D. BELL, M.A., Honorary Canon of Carlisle. Crown 8vo, 5s., cloth.

"We express our sincere hope that such an able and excellent course of lectures may have a wide circulation."—*Record.*

LETTERS OF RUTH BRYAN. By the Author of "Handfuls of Purpose." With a Preface by the Rev. A. MOODY STUART, M.A. New Edition. Crown 8vo, 5s., cloth.

"Ruth Bryan's letters are remarkably like Samuel Rutherford's, not rivalling them in depth, and genius, and sanctified wit sublimed into heavenly imagery, but closely resembling them in most winning, unwearied, and gloriously endless eulogy of the King in his beauty."—*Extract from Preface.*

DARE TO DO RIGHT. By the Author of "Nettie's Mission," &c. With coloured Illustrations. Crown 8vo, 3s. 6d., cloth.

"We have seldom met with a volume so thoroughly suited to boyish tastes, and so well calculated to exercise a good influence over young readers."—*Leeds Mercury.*

LECTURES ON GREAT MEN. By the late Rev. FREDERIC MYERS, M.A. With Preface by the Rev. T. H. TARLTON. Sixth Edition. Crown 8vo, 5s., cloth.

"Admirable lectures, true, sterling, thorough."—*Watchman.*

A GOLDEN SUNSET. An account of the last days of Hannah Broomfield. By the Rev. J. R. MACDUFF, D.D., Author of "The Gates of Prayer," &c. 16mo, 1s. 6d., cloth.

"As a present for servants the book is especially valuable; but few masters or mistresses could read it without pleasure or profit."—*Christian.*

CHRIST AND THE CHURCH. Sermons on the Apostolic Commission. (Matt. xxviii. 18-20.) By the Rev. ADOLPH SAPHIR, B.A. Crown 8vo, 6s., cloth.

"Eloquent, beautiful, and profoundly evangelical sermons."—*Literary World.*

SELECT REMAINS OF ISLAY BURNS, D.D., of the Free Church College, Glasgow. Edited by the Rev. JAMES C. BURNS. With Memoir by the Rev. Professor BLAIKIE, D.D. Post 8vo, 7s. 6d. cloth.

"A varied and most instructive volume."—*Weekly Review.*

CROSSING THE RIVER. By the Author of "The Life of the late Rev. Dr. Marsh," "Memorials of Capt. Hedley Vicars," &c. Crown 8vo, 1s. cloth limp.

"This little volume is perhaps the most beautiful and touching of all that Miss Marsh has written."—*Preacher's Lantern.*

RELIGIOUS POEMS. By the Author of "Stepping Heavenward," &c. Crown 8vo, 3s. 6d., cloth.

"A volume of very sweet poems couched in a truly devotional spirit."—*Weekly Review.*

THE TRIUMPH OF FAITH. The Substance of Addresses on the Book of Joshua. By STEVENSON A. BLACKWOOD. Crown 8vo, 2s. cloth limp; 2s. 6d. boards.

"It is distinguished by thoughtful exposition, and a deeply religious tone pervades every page."—*Watchman.*

LONG EVENINGS, AND WORK TO DO IN THEM. By Mrs. BAYLY, Author of "Ragged homes, and how to mend them." Crown 8vo, 4s. 6d. cloth.

"After an introduction full of incident and descriptive of work, follows a series of chapters on Wycliffe, Tyndale, and Gutenberg, which are written with great spirit, discrimination, and clearness."—*British Quarterly Review.*

CHURCH AND HOME LESSONS FROM THE BOOK OF HOSEA, FOR FAMILY READING. By the Rev. A. C. THISELTON, Dublin. Crown 8vo, 5s., cloth.

"The style of these addresses is earnest and practical, and we have pleasure in recommending them."—*Church of England Magazine.*

THE RELATIONS OF THE KINGDOM TO THE WORLD. By the Rev. J. OSWALD DYKES, D.D. Author of "The Beatitudes of the Kingdom," &c. Crown 8vo, 3s. 6d. cloth.

"For a certain nervous clearness of style, delightful freshness and vigour of thought, he has few equals in the Presbyterian Church."—*North British Daily Mail.*

THE CHURCH IN THE HOUSE. A Series of Lessons on the Acts of the Apostles. By the Rev. WILLIAM ARNOT, Edinburgh, Author of "This Present World," &c. Post 8vo, 7s. 6d. cloth.

"Racy and readable, based upon solid study, and brightened with facts gathered by an unusually observant eye, and with the fancies of an active imagination."—*British and Foreign Evangelical Review.*

THE HEALING WATERS OF ISRAEL; or, The Story of Naaman the Syrian. An Old Testament Chapter in Providence and Grace. By the Rev. J. R. MACDUFF, D.D., Author of "Memories of Bethany." Crown 8vo, 4s. 6d. cloth.

"Told with all his vigorous power of enforcing Scripture truth, and bringing it home to the heart and conscience. It teaches, in a striking manner, many most useful lessons."—*Christian Observer*.

DARK SAYINGS OF OLD. Being an attempt to Elucidate certain Difficult Passages of Holy Scripture, in a Series of Ten Lectures. By the Rev. J. B. McCAUL, Honorary Canon of Rochester, &c. Post 8vo, 5s. cloth.

"A valuable contribution to current theological literature, and well adapted to counteract some of those erroneous opinions on sacred subjects which are sadly too prevalent in the present day."—*Church of England Magazine*.

THE GATES OF PRAYER. A Book of Private Devotion for Morning and Evening. By the Author of "Morning and Night Watches." 16mo, 2s. cloth.

"The prayers of which this volume is composed are of a high order, and will be found full of suggestions."—*Rock*.

BLACK IVORY. A Tale of Adventure among the Slavers of East Africa. By R. M. BALLANTYNE, Author of "The Lifeboat," "The Norsemen in the West," &c. Illustrations. Second Edition. Crown 8vo, 5s. cloth.

"A captivating story, and likely to do good withal, with incident and information, the picturesque and the practical, adventure and pathetic appeals, skilfully mingled for a good purpose."—*Record*.

UNDER THE SURFACE. Poems by FRANCES RIDLEY HAVERGAL, Author of "The Ministry of Song," &c. Crown 8vo, 5s. cloth.

"Great freshness of feeling, fulness of thought, and ready command of measure."—*British Quarterly Review*.

THE WORD OF LIFE. Being Selections from the Work of a Ministry. By the Rev. CHARLES J. BROWN, D.D., Edinburgh. Post 8vo, 6s. cloth.

"Good specimens of the higher class of sermons given from the Scottish pulpit." —*Edinburgh Courant*.

THE GOSPEL AND ITS FRUITS. A Book for the Young. By the Rev. J. H. WILSON, Edinburgh, Author of "Our Father in Heaven," &c. Crown 8vo, 3s. 6d. cloth.

"The book is quite unique. Full of sound doctrinal teaching, illustrated by anecdote and hymn and picture, it commands and rivets attention."—*Daily Review*.

TALES OF ADVENTURE ON THE SEA, AND TALES OF ADVENTURE BY FLOOD, FIELD, AND MOUNTAIN. From "Ballantyne's Miscellany." By R. M. BALLANTYNE, Author of "The Lighthouse," &c. With Illustrations by the Author. Crown 8vo, each 3s. 6d. cloth.

"A better prize for the deserving school-boy could not be found than this pleasant-looking book full of seafaring experience and tales of heroism."—*English Independent on Volume I.*

THE MINISTRY OF SONG. By FRANCES RIDLEY HAVERGAL, Author of "Bruey," &c. Cheaper Edition. 32mo, 1s. 6d. cloth.

"Exquisite poems."—*Our Own Fireside.*

"Full of real poetry—rich, deep, true, sweet, and brave thoughts."—*Woman's Work.*

MEMOIR OF THE REV. J. J. WEITBRECHT, Late Missionary of the Church Missionary Society in Bengal. Compiled by his WIDOW from his Journals and his Letters. With a Preface by the late Rev. H. VENN, M.A. Cheaper Edition. Crown 8vo, 3s. 6d. cloth.

"The book ought to have a place in every library that has a missionary department."—*Literary World.*

OUR FRIENDS IN HEAVEN; or, The Mutual Recognition of the Redeemed in Glory Demonstrated. By the Rev. J. M. KILLEN, D.D., Author of "Our Companions in Glory," &c. Fifteenth Edition. Crown 8vo, 3s. 6d. cloth.

"A full, earnest, and conclusive investigation of the entire subject."—*British and Foreign Evangelical Review.*

LIGHT AND LIFE IN CHRIST. By the Rev. F. WHITFIELD, M.A., Author of "Voices from the Valley," "Earthly Shadows of the Heavenly Kingdom," &c. Crown 8vo, 5s. cloth.

"A series of expositions fresh in thought, spiritual in tone, and warm in feeling." —*Our Own Fireside.*

CHILD LIFE. A Collection of Poems. Edited by JOHN GREENLEAF WHITTIER. With many Illustrations. 4to, 6s. cloth, gilt edges.

"Turning over its leaves, it appears to us a charming volume, and we know of no other which strings together so many gems of the like water."—*Times.*

SOLDIERS AND SERVANTS OF CHRIST: or, Chapters on Church History. With Preface by the Rev. F. V. MATHER, M.A., Vicar of St. Paul's, Clifton, and Canon of Bristol. Second Edition. Crown 8vo, 5s. cloth.

"An exceedingly valuable book. . . . The narratives embrace chief names from the 1st to the 16th century, and are so told that they will interest young people." —*Christian Observer.*

SERMONS AND LECTURES. By the late Rev. JAMES HAMILTON, D.D., F.L.S., Author of "Life in Earnest," "The Great Biography," &c. Post 8vo, 7s. 6d. cloth.

"A number of sermons and lectures, in all cases, of extreme beauty and excellence." —*Rock.*

QUESTIONS OF THE DAY. By the Rev. JOHN HALL, D.D., of New York, late of Dublin. Crown 8vo, 4s. 6d. cloth.

"A volume of admirable papers, full of acute thinking, attractively expressed. A section would make admirable fireside reading in the family."—*British and Foreign Evangelical Review.*

THIS PRESENT WORLD. Sketches from Nature and Art, taken in the Vacations of a Professional Life. By the Rev. WILLIAM ARNOT, Edinburgh, Author of "The Parables of our Lord." Crown 8vo, 3s. 6d. cloth.

"A delightful little book, and one likely, we think, to be very useful."—*Edinburgh Courant.*

SERMONS ON OLD TESTAMENT SUBJECTS. By the late Rev. EDWARD WALKER, D.C.L., Rector of Cheltenham. Edited by the Rev. T. P. BOULTBEE, LL.D. Crown 8vo, 5s. cloth.

"Full of sound Gospel truth, these sermons are marked by great earnestness and directness of appeal."—*Rock.*

CHRIST CRUCIFIED. Lectures on 1 Corinthians ii. By the Rev. ADOLPH SAPHIR, B.A. Crown 8vo, 3s. 6d. cloth.

"A valuable commentary."—*Sword and Trowel.*

"An earnest, forcible, luminous presentation of the mind of the Spirit."—*Literary World.*

VOICES FROM THE VALLEY TESTIFYING OF JESUS. By the Rev. F. WHITFIELD, M.A., author of "Earthly Shadows of the Heavenly Kingdom," &c. Seventh Edition, Small Crown 8vo, 3s. 6d. cloth.

"Eloquent, evangelical and simple, we cannot express too high an opinion of these expositions of Scripture."—*Our Own Fireside.*

THE NORSEMEN IN THE WEST; or, America before Columbus. By R. M. BALLANTYNE, author of "The Iron Horse," &c. Crown 8vo, 5s. cloth, with Illustrations.

"A book that cannot possibly be laid down till the very last word of the last line has been read."—*Athenæum.*

THE LAWS OF THE KINGDOM. By the Rev. J. OSWALD DYKES, D.D., Author of "The Beatitudes of the Kingdom." Second Edition, Crown 8vo, 3s. 6d. cloth.

"An expositor worthy of the theme . . . . We recommend the book heartily."—*Edinburgh Courant.*

SYNOPTICAL LECTURES ON THE BOOKS OF HOLY SCRIPTURE. First Series—Genesis to Song of Songs—Second Series—Isaiah to Acts. By the Rev. DONALD FRASER, D.D., Marylebone. Crown 8vo, each 6s. cloth.

"Singularly interesting, instructive and comprehensive lectures."—*Record.*

SCRIPTURE ITSELF THE ILLUSTRATOR. A Manual of Illustrations, gathered from Scriptural Figures, Phrases, Types, Derivations, Chronology, Texts, etc., adapted for the use of Preachers and Teachers. By the Rev. G. S. BOWES, B.A. Small Crown 8vo, 3s. 6d. cloth.

"Evidently the result of attentive and persevering study . . . . We strongly recommend it to the notice of preachers and teachers, feeling sure that they will derive many suggestive hints from it."—*Church of England Magazine.*

BRUEY, A LITTLE WORKER FOR CHRIST. By FRANCES RIDLEY HAVERGAL, Author of "The Ministry of Song." Third Edition, Small Crown 8vo, 3s. 6d. cloth.

"Written in a fascinating style."—*Woman's Work.*
"A peculiarly interesting volume."—*Churchman's Shilling Magazine.*

PAPERS FOR HOME READING. By the Rev. JOHN HALL, D.D., New York. Second Edition, Small Crown 8vo, 3s. 6d. cloth.

"Lively, practical, and earnest, and on themes of the deepest moment."—*English Independent.*
"The whole collection is excellent."—*Presbyterian.*

THE DEATH OF SELF, THE LIFE OF SERVICE. Lectures on Isaiah vi., preached in Portman Chapel, during Lent, 1872. By the Rev. J. W. REEVE, M.A. Small Crown 8vo, 3s. 6d. cloth.

"Weighty truths expressed with much earnestness and plainness."—*Church of England Magazine.*
"Can hardly be too fervently commended to the attention of the Christian reader."—*Record.*

THE BEATITUDES OF THE KINGDOM. By the Rev. J. OSWALD DYKES, D.D. Third Edition. Small Crown 8vo, 3s. 6d. cloth.

"The purity of Mr. Dykes's language and the lucidity of thought and expression, combine to render this one of the choicest contributions to Christology which we have lately met with."—*Nonconformist.*

MOSES THE MAN OF GOD. A Series of Lectures by the late JAMES HAMILTON, D.D., F.L.S. Third Edition. Small Crown 8vo, 5s., cloth.

"Graceful description, imaginative reconstruction, unconventional, and often very ingenious, sometimes learned disquisition, with the light graceful touch of poetic style and delicate fancy."—*British Quarterly Review.*

LAYS OF THE HOLY LAND. Selected from Ancient and Modern Poets by the Rev. HORATIUS BONAR, D.D. New Edition, with Illustrations from original Photographs and Drawings. Crown 4to, 12s., cloth.

"The Holy Land is a subject to which all great poets have devoted some of their best endeavours, and these are now brought together and adorned by illustrations worthy of such a text. . . . The volume will long remain a favourite."—*Times.*

THE FLOATING LIGHT OF THE GOODWIN SANDS. A Tale by R. M. BALLANTYNE, Author of "The Lifeboat," &c. With Illustrations. Crown 8vo, 5s. cloth.

"As full of incident, as healthy in tone, and as fresh and vigorous in style as any of its predecessors."—*Scotsman.*

THE LIFE OF THE LATE JAMES HAMILTON, D.D., F.L.S. By the Rev. WILLIAM ARNOT, Edinburgh. Post 8vo, 7s. 6d. cloth. With Portrait.

"We rejoice to recommend this volume as a congenial and worthy record of one of the noblest and most fruitful lives with which the Church of Christ has been blessed in modern days. The editor's work has been done with admirable judgment." —*Weekly Review.*

A MEMOIR OF THE LATE REV. WILLIAM C. BURNS, M.A., Missionary to China. By the late Professor ISLAY BURNS, D.D., Glasgow. Crown 8vo, 6s. cloth. With Portrait. Cheap Edition. Small Crown 8vo, 3s. 6d. cloth.

"A more apostolic life has rarely been spent. . . . It is impossible to estimate too highly the good that may flow from this record of Christian life and labour." —*Sunday Magazine.*

THE LORD'S PRAYER. Lectures by the Rev. ADOLPH SAPHIR, B.A., Greenwich. Fifth Edition. Small Crown 8vo, 5s. cloth.

"A work so wide in its range of thought, and so concentrated in its doctrinal teachings, so rich and well packed, yet so simple and interesting, and so clear, pure, and intelligible in expression does not often make its appearance."—*Christian Work.*

BLENDING LIGHTS; or, The Relations of Natural Science, Archæology, and History to the Bible. By the Rev. WILLIAM FRASER, LL.D. Second Edition. Post 8vo, 6s. 6d. cloth.

"Before dismissing this particular subject allow me, with all earnestness and most grateful thanks to the author, to draw special attention to a truly admirable recently published volume on the Relations of Natural Science to the Bible, by the Rev. Dr. Fraser, of Paisley."—*Address by Dr. Duff as Moderator of the Free General Assembly.*

SERMONS. Preached at King's Lynn. By the late Rev. E. L. HULL, B.A. First, Second, and Third Series. Post 8vo, each 6s. cloth.

"This new volume of twenty sermons has all the claims of the first—the same happy use of Scripture, the same clear and firm grasp of the principle of every text he selected, the same earnest longing after the beauty and holiness on which he has now entered, the same play of imagination, the same freshness of thought, and fitness of utterance."—*Freeman on Second Series.*

BOOKS FOR WAYFARERS. By ANNA WARNER, Author of the "Golden Ladder." 32mo, cloth. 1. WAYFARING HYMNS, ORIGINAL AND SELECTED. 6d. 2. THE MELODY OF THE TWENTY-THIRD PSALM. 8d. 3. THE OTHER SHORE. 1s. 4. THE FOURTH WATCH. 10d.

"There is an unction and a beauty about the books that well fit them to be pocket or table companions."—*Freeman.*

"Two little books, beautiful without and within."—*English Presbyterian Messenger.*

MEMORIALS OF THE LATE JAMES HENDERSON, M.D., F.R.C.S.E., Medical Missionary to China. With Appendix. Seventh Edition. Small Crown 8vo, 3s. 6d. cloth. With Portrait. Also, Cheap and Abridged Edition, 16mo, 1s. cloth limp.

"The memorials of Dr. Henderson form as beautiful and exhilarating a little history as it has been for some time our task or pleasure to read. . . . . It is the story of one of those noble lives before which power and difficulty recoil, and give up the contest."—*Eclectic Review.*

DEEP DOWN. A Tale of the Cornish Mines. By R. M. BALLANTYNE, Author of "The Life-Boat," etc. With Illustrations. Small Crown 8vo, 5s. cloth.

"This is just the subject for Mr. Ballantyne, whose stories in connection with that enterprise and adventure which have made England great are amongst the best of modern days."—*Daily News.*

THE WORKS OF THE LATE JAMES HAMILTON, D.D., F.L.S. Complete in Six Vols., Post 8vo, each 7s. 6d. cloth.

"More than most men he has embalmed his qualities in his writings. . . They well deserve to be published in a permanent form, and this handsome library edition will be a great boon to many families."—*Freeman.*

ENGLISH HEARTS AND ENGLISH HANDS; or, The Railway and the Trenches. By the Author of "Memorials of Captain Hedley Vicars." Small Crown 8vo, 5s. cloth. Also a Cheaper Edition, 2s. cloth limp.

"The Memorials of Vicars and these Memorials of the Crystal Palace Navvies are books of precisely the same type, and must not be overlooked. We recognize in them an honesty of purpose, a purity of heart, and a warmth of human affection, combined with a religious faith, that are very beautiful."—*Times.*

THE EXETER HALL LECTURES TO YOUNG MEN, from their commencement in 1845-6, to their termination in 1864-5, all uniformly printed, and handsomely bound in cloth, and embellished with portraits of the Friends and Patrons of the Young Men's Christian Association. Complete in 20 vols., price of each volume, 4s.; or the whole series for £3.

THE REV. THOS. SCOTT'S COMMENTARY ON THE HOLY BIBLE, comprising Marginal References, a copious Topical Index, Fifteen Maps, and Sixty-nine Engravings, illustrative of Scripture Incidents and Scenery. Complete in 6 vols. 4to, published at £4 4s., now offered for £2 10s.

THE BIBLE MANUAL: an Expository and Practical Commentary on the Books of Scripture, arranged in Chronological Order: forming a Hand-book of Biblical Elucidation for the use of Families, Schools, and Students of the Word of God. Translated from the German Work, edited by the late Rev. Dr. C. G. BARTH, of Calw, Wurtemberg. Third Edition. Imperial 8vo, 12s. cloth.

MATTHEW HENRY'S COMMENTARY ON THE HOLY BIBLE, comprising upwards of 7000 Pages, well printed (the Notes as well as the Text in clear and distinct type) on good paper, forming Nine Imperial 8vo volumes, and handsomely bound in cloth. Price £3 3s.

*** The work may also be had in a variety of extra bindings, particulars of which will be forwarded on application.

THE WORD SERIES.

By ELIZABETH WETHERALL and ANNA LOTHROP, Authors of "The Wide Wide World." With Coloured Illustrations. Crown 8vo, each 3s. 6d. cloth.

1. WALKS FROM EDEN: The Scripture Story from the Creation to the Death of Abraham.

2. THE HOUSE OF ISRAEL: The Scripture Story from the Birth of Isaac to the Death of Jacob.

3. THE STAR OUT OF JACOB: The Scripture Story Illustrating the Earlier Portion of the Gospel Narrative.

THE GOLDEN LADDER SERIES.

Uniform in size and binding, with coloured Illustrations. Crown 8vo, cloth.

1. THE GOLDEN LADDER: Stories Illustrative of the Eight Beatitudes. By ELIZABETH and ANNA WARNER. 3s. 6d.
2. THE WIDE WIDE WORLD. By ELIZABETH WARNER. 3s. 6d.
3. QUEECHY. By the same. 3s. 6d.
4. MELBOURNE HOUSE. By the same. 3s. 6d.
5. DAISY. By the same. 3s. 6d.
6. THE OLD HELMET. By the same. 3s. 6d.
7. THE THREE LITTLE SPADES. By the same. 2s. 6d.
8. NETTIE'S MISSION: Stories Illustrative of the Lord's Prayer. By ALICE GRAY. 3s. 6d.
9. DAISY IN THE FIELD. By ELIZABETH WARNER. 3s. 6d.
10. STEPPING HEAVENWARD. By Mrs. PRENTISS. Author of "Little Susy." 2s. 6d.
11. WHAT SHE COULD, AND OPPORTUNITIES. Tales by ELIZABETH WARNER. 3s. 6d.
12. GLEN LUNA. By ANNA WARNER. 3s. 6d.
13. DRAYTON HALL. Stories Illustrative of the Beatitudes. By ALICE GRAY. 3s. 6d.
14. WITHOUT AND WITHIN. A New England Story. 3s. 6d.
15. VINEGAR HILL STORIES. Illustrative of the Parable of the Sower. By ANNA WARNER. 3s. 6d.
16. LITTLE SUNBEAMS. By J. H. MATTHEWS. 3s. 6d.
17. THE HOUSE IN TOWN AND TRADING. 3s. 6d.
18. THE LITTLE CAMP ON EAGLE HILL. By ELIZABETH WARNER. 3s. 6d.
19. WILLOW BROOK. By the Author of "The Wide Wide World." 3s. 6d.
20. DARE TO DO RIGHT. By the Author of "Nettie's Mission." 3s. 6d.
21. SCEPTRES AND CROWNS AND THE FLAG OF TRUCE. Tales. By the Author of "The Wide Wide World." 3s. 6d.
22. URBANÉ AND HIS FRIENDS. By the Author of "Stepping Heavenward." 2s. 6d.

THE SELECT SERIES.

Crown 8vo, each 3s. 6d. cloth. Bound by BURN. Most of them with Illustrations.

1. DERRY. A Tale of the Revolution. By CHARLOTTE ELIZABETH.
2. THE LAND OF THE FORUM AND THE VATICAN. By the Rev. NEWMAN HALL, LL.B.
3. THE LISTENER. By CAROLINE FRY.
4. DAYS AND NIGHTS IN THE EAST; or, Illustrations of Bible Scenes. By the Rev. HORATIUS BONAR, D.D.
5. THE HOLY WAR. By JOHN BUNYAN.
6. THE PILGRIM'S PROGRESS. By JOHN BUNYAN.
7. THE MOUNTAINS OF THE BIBLE; Their Scenes and their Lessons. By the Rev. JOHN MACFARLANE, LL.D.
8. HOME AND FOREIGN SERVICE; or, Pictures in Active Christian Life.
9. LIFE. A Series of Illustrations of the Divine Wisdom in the Forms, Structures, and Instincts of Animals. By PHILLIP H. GOSSE, F.R.S.
10. LAND AND SEA. By P. H. GOSSE, F.R.S.
11. JOHN KNOX AND HIS TIMES. By the Author of "The Story of Martin Luther," etc.
12. HOME IN THE HOLY LAND. By Mrs. FINN.
13. A THIRD YEAR IN JERUSALEM. A Tale Illustrating Incidents and Customs in Modern Jerusalem. By Mrs. FINN.

14 & 15. THE ROMANCE OF NATURAL HISTORY. By P. H. GOSSE, F.R.S. First and Second Series.

16. BYEWAYS IN PALESTINE. By JAMES FINN, Esq. F.R.A.S., late H. M. Consul of Jerusalem and Palestine.
17. BLOOMFIELD. A Tale by ELIZABETH WARREN, Author of "John Knox and his Times," &c.
18. TALES FROM ALSACE; or, Scenes and Portraits from Life in the Days of the Reformation, as drawn from old Chronicles. Translated from the German.
19. HYMNS OF THE CHURCH MILITANT. Edited by the Author of "The Wide Wide World."
20. THE PHYSICIAN'S DAUGHTERS; or, The Spring Time of Woman. By the Author of "Wandering Homes and their Influences," &c.
21. WANDERING HOMES AND THEIR INFLUENCES. By the author of "The Physician's Daughters."

-rson, Rait, & Fenton, Printers, 69, Marylebone Lane, Oxford Street.